MACHINE LEARNING
DATA TO DECISION

SACHIN DAVE

Contents

"To my mother, Dr. Harshida Dave, sanskrit scholar. Since childhood we have seen her doing academic research, UGC fellowship, and work on difficult areas of manuscriptology which have been my foundation.

Preface

For over three decades, I have had the privilege of working at the intersection of technology, leadership, and innovation. My journey in the world of Information Technology has been shaped by roles at some of the industry's leading organizations, including Barclays, Infosys Technologies, and Wipro Technologies. As an Associate Vice President of Technology, Technology Architect, Software Engineering Lead, and a passionate mentor for STEM initiatives, I've experienced firsthand how technology can drive business transformation, solve complex problems, and create new opportunities for individuals and organizations alike.

Throughout my career, I've had the opportunity to lead teams of talented engineers and architects, working on a diverse array of projects across industries ranging from banking and finance to global IT services. At Barclays, I honed my skills in leading enterprise-wide technology initiatives and managing mission-critical systems. At Infosys Technologies and Wipro Technologies, I deepened my understanding of the global IT landscape, architecting solutions for clients worldwide and delivering innovative software engineering solutions that addressed the unique needs of each organization.

As an advocate for STEM education and a mentor to aspiring technologists, I have also seen the immense value in nurturing the next generation of leaders and innovators. My work with STEM initiatives at

Barclays has been a rewarding part of my career, where I've had the privilege of guiding young minds, encouraging them to explore the vast potential of technology, and empowering them to chart their own paths in a rapidly evolving field.

This book is a culmination of my experiences, both as a technologist and as a mentor for the next generation of STEM leaders. I've seen how young minds, when given the right tools and guidance, can unlock new possibilities in the world of machine learning and data science. It is my hope that this book will not only serve as a guide for current professionals in the field but also inspire aspiring technologists to embrace the challenges and opportunities that lie ahead in the world of machine learning.

In the following chapters, we will explore the key concepts behind machine learning algorithms, delve into real-world applications, and discuss how these algorithms can be used to extract value from data in ways that drive smarter decisions. From supervised learning to deep learning, we will look at how each technique can be applied to real-world problems, providing the reader with both a theoretical foundation and practical knowledge that can be implemented in their own work.

Machine learning is no longer a futuristic concept—it is here, shaping the decisions we make every day. The algorithms that power it are at the core of transforming data into decisions. As technology continues to evolve, the demand for expertise in this field will only grow, and it is my hope that this book will equip you with the knowledge and inspiration to lead in this exciting space.

Thank you for joining me on this exploration of machine learning, data-driven decision-making, and the algorithms that are revolutionizing industries. I am excited to share the lessons learned and insights gained over my career and to guide you on your own journey in the world of machine learning and technology.

Acknowledgments

Writing this book demanded significant effort and countless late nights. I would like to express my gratitude to everyone who discussed, and motivated me to the creation of Machine Learning Data to Decisions.

This book would not have been possible without the support, encouragement from my friends and family members. Especially coming from an engineering background with 25+ Years dedicated to Information Technology and continuous learning, I never thought I could come up with a book.

My son Yash Dave, 10th grader at Governor Livingston Highschool inspired me for the overall journey of the book, he took enormous interest in upcoming technology trends, a lot of Q&A sessions and curiosity.

A heartfelt thanks to the editorial team, designers, and publishers at *The Paper House*, who helped bring this book to life. Their professionalism, attention to detail, and commitment to excellence made this entire process smooth and enjoyable.

Finally, I would like to dedicate this book to those who are just beginning their journey in the world of data science and machine learning. May the tools and techniques presented here help you make informed decisions and inspire future innovations.

Thank you all for being part of this exciting endeavor.

About the Author

With over three decades of experience in Information Technology, **Sachin Dave** has held key leadership roles, including Associate Vice President at Barclays. Having worked with industry giants like Infosys and Wipro Technology, I have witnessed and contributed to the IT evolution from the Y2K era to the rise of AI and Machine Learning. A passionate STEM mentor, Sachin Dave is dedicated to fostering the next generation of tech leaders. My extensive expertise spans diverse domains, from banking solutions to cutting-edge innovations. This book is a reflection of my journey and insights into the ever-evolving world of technology.

Data To Decision using Machine Learning

Electronic data is generated every day in the modern world. It is persisted and accessed by various applications and business platforms for business processes, business analytics, business reporting, trending, and forecasting. We will understand how machine learning is used to solve real-world problems in different domains, covering a few examples: e-commerce, the Energy sector, Finance, Insurance, IT Systems, Markets, Medical Science, retail, science, and the Social World.

Application platforms use structured information or non-structured information and have various options for storing and retrieving the info including DBMS (Database management systems), RDMS (Relational database management system), Bigdata platforms, Cache databases, file systems, record management systems, etc. on premise or cloud hosted.

To enable enterprise platforms with **real-time analytics**, **data prediction,** and **AI based decision**-making processes, it is important to understand a wide variety of machine learning techniques.

Machine learning (ML) is a powerful technique for making data-based decisions. Here's a general overview of how data is processed to make decisions using ML:

1. **Data Collection**: Gather relevant data from various sources. This could be anything from customer transactions and sensor readings to social media interactions.

2. **Data Preparation**: Clean and preprocess the data. This involves handling missing values, removing duplicates, normalizing or standardizing data, and transforming features. Proper data preparation is crucial for building an effective ML model.
3. **Exploratory Data Analysis (EDA)**: Analyze the data to understand its characteristics and uncover patterns or relationships. EDA helps in selecting appropriate features and understanding the underlying trends.
4. **Feature Engineering**: Create new features or modify existing ones to improve the model's performance. This could involve selecting relevant features, creating interaction terms, or deriving new variables from existing ones.
5. **Model Selection**: Choose an appropriate machine learning algorithm based on the problem type (e.g., classification, regression, clustering). Common algorithms include linear regression, decision trees, support vector machines, and neural networks.
6. **Model Training**: Use the prepared data to train the ML model. This involves feeding the data into the algorithm and adjusting the model's parameters to minimize error and improve accuracy.
7. **Model Evaluation**: Assess the model's performance using metrics such as accuracy, precision, recall, F1 score, or mean squared error, depending on the problem type. Validation techniques like cross- validation help evaluate how well the model generalizes to unseen data.
8. **Hyperparameter Tuning**: Optimize the model's hyperparameters to enhance performance. This can be done using techniques like grid search or random search.
9. **Prediction**: Use the trained model to make predictions on new, unseen data. These predictions can be used to inform decisions.
10. **Decision Making**: Based on the model's predictions, make informed decisions. For instance, if a model predicts that a customer is likely to churn, a company might decide to offer them a retention deal.
11. **Model Monitoring and Maintenance**: Continuously monitor the model's performance over time. As new data comes in or business conditions change, retrain or adjust the model to maintain its effectiveness.
12. **Feedback Loop**: Incorporate feedback from decision outcomes

to refine the model and improve future predictions. This helps in adapting to new trends or changes in the data.

By following these steps, machine learning can transform raw data into actionable insights, enabling more informed and effective decision-making.

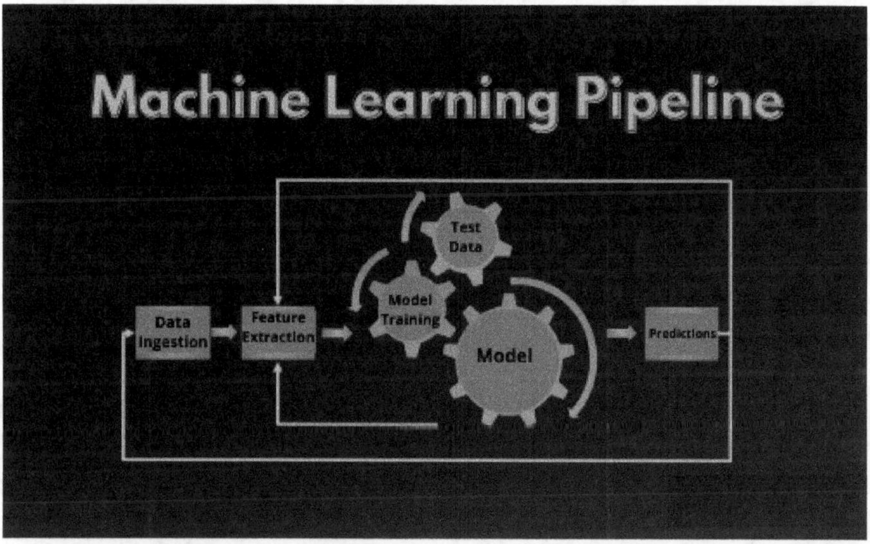

Tools and Techniques

- **Pandas, NumPy:** For data manipulation and analysis.
- **Matplotlib, Seaborn:** For data visualization.
- **Scikit-learn:** For splitting data, encoding features, and other preprocessing tasks.

Understanding your data thoroughly helps ensure that you can build robust machine-learning models and make informed decisions based on the data's characteristics and quality.

ML Algorithms used at each stage of data to decisions

Algorithmic Approaches	ML Step	Goal / Problem type
PCA	Data Understanding	Dimensionality Reduction
Topic Model	Data Understanding	Clustering
K-Means	Data Understating	Clustering
Linear Regression	Prediction	Regression
Lasso Regression (L1)	Prediction	Regression
Ridge Regression (L2)	Prediction	Regression
Logistic Regression	Prediction	Classification
LDA (Linear Discriminant Analysis)	Prediction	Classification
QDA (Quadratic Discriminant Analysis)	Prediction	Classification
KNN (K-Nearest Neighbors)	Prediction	Classification / Regression
Neural Networks	Prediction	Classification / Regression
Reinforcement Learning	Decision Making	Hybrid/Multiple
Multi-Armed Bandit	Decision Making	Hybrid/Multiple
Markov Decision Process (MDP)	Decision Making	Hybrid/Multiple
Model Predictive Control	Decision Making	Hybrid/Multiple
Randomized Control	Causal Inferences	Experimentation
Synthetic Control	Causal Inferences	Experimentation

Principal Component Analysis (PCA)

Principal Component Analysis (PCA) is a widely used dimensionality reduction technique in machine learning and data analysis. It transforms high-dimensional data into a lower-dimensional form while preserving as much variance (information) as possible. Here's a comprehensive overview of PCA:

1. Concept and Purpose

- **Dimensionality Reduction:** PCA reduces the number of features while retaining the most significant variance in the dataset.
- **Data Visualization:** It helps visualize high-dimensional data in 2D or 3D by projecting it onto principal components.
- **Noise Reduction:** PCA can help in reducing noise and improving the performance of machine learning algorithms by focusing on the most informative features.

2. How PCA Works

1. **Standardization:**

- **Standardize the Data:** PCA is sensitive to the scale of the features. Standardize the features to have mean zero and variance one if they are on different scales.

```
from sklearn.preprocessing import StandardScaler
scaler = StandardScaler()
standardized_data = scaler.fit_transform(data)
```

2. **Compute Covariance Matrix:**

- **Covariance Matrix:** Calculate the covariance matrix to understand the relationships between different features.

```
import numpy as np
covariance_matrix = np.cov(standardized_data.T)
```

3. **Compute Eigenvalues and Eigenvectors:**

- **Eigen Decomposition:** Compute the eigenvalues and eigenvectors of the covariance matrix. Eigenvectors represent the directions of maximum variance (principal components), and eigenvalues represent the magnitude of the variance.

```
eig_vals, eig_vecs = np.linalg.eig(covariance_matrix)
```

4. **Sort Eigenvalues and Eigenvectors:**

- **Sort:** Sort the eigenvalues and corresponding eigenvectors in descending order. The eigenvectors with the largest eigenvalues represent the principal components.

```
sorted_indices = np.argsort(eig_vals)[::-1]
sorted_eig_vecs = eig_vecs[:, sorted_indices]
```

5. **Select Top Components:**

- **Select Components:** Choose the top k eigenvectors (principal components) based on the desired number of dimensions or explained variance.

```
k = 2  # Number of principal components to keep
top_eig_vecs = sorted_eig_vecs[:, :k]
```

6. **Transform Data:**

- **Project Data:** Transform the original data into the new space defined by the principal components.

```
transformed_data = standardized_data.dot(top_eig_vecs)
```

3. PCA in Python

```
from sklearn.decomposition import PCA
from sklearn.preprocessing import StandardScaler

# Standardize the data
scaler = StandardScaler()
standardized_data = scaler.fit_transform(data)

# Apply PCA
pca = PCA(n_components=2)  # Reduce to 2 dimensions
principal_components = pca.fit_transform(standardized_data)

# The resulting principal_components can be used for visualization or further analysis
```

4. Interpreting PCA Results

- **Explained Variance:** Each principal component captures a certain amount of the total variance. The sum of the explained variances of the selected components should give you an idea of how much of the original variance is retained.

```
explained_variance_ratio = pca.explained_variance_ratio_
```

- **Scree Plot:** A scree plot helps determine the number of principal components to retain. It plots the eigenvalues in descending order.

5. Applications

- **Data Preprocessing:** PCA is often used as a preprocessing step to reduce the dimensionality of the dataset before applying machine learning algorithms.
- **Data Visualization:** PCA helps visualize high-dimensional data by projecting it onto two or three principal components.
- **Noise Reduction:** It can help in denoising the data by keeping the most significant components and discarding the noise-related components.

6. Limitations

- **Linearity:** PCA assumes linear relationships between features. It may not capture non-linear relationships effectively.
- **Interpretability:** The principal components are linear combinations of the original features, which may not always be easy to interpret.

PCA is a powerful tool for dimensionality reduction and feature extraction, and understanding its mechanics can greatly enhance your data analysis and machine learning workflows.

Topic modeling

Topic modeling is a technique in machine learning and natural language processing (NLP) used to discover the underlying topics in a collection of documents. It helps in understanding the themes and patterns within text data, making it useful for organizing, summarizing, and finding insights in large text corpora. Here's a detailed overview of topic modeling techniques:

1. Concept of Topic Modeling

- **Objective:** Topic modeling aims to identify topics or themes in a text corpus by analyzing word co- occurrences and patterns. Each document is assumed to be a mixture of topics, and each topic is characterized by a distribution of words.

2. Common Topic Modeling Techniques

2.1. Latent Dirichlet Allocation (LDA)

- **Overview:**
  - LDA is one of the most popular topic modeling techniques. It assumes each document is generated by a mixture of topics and each topic is generated by a mixture of words.

  - LDA uses a generative probabilistic model to infer the topics from the documents.

- **How It Works:**
  - **Define the Number of Topics:** Set the number of topics you want to extract.
  - **Initialize Topics:** Randomly assign words in documents to topics.
  - **Iterate:** Update topic assignments based on the probability distributions of words in topics and documents in topics.
  - **Convergence:** Repeat the iterations until the model converges to stable topic assignments.
  - **Implementation:**

```
from sklearn.decomposition import LatentDirichletAllocation
from sklearn.feature_extraction.text import CountVectorizer

# Prepare the text data
vectorizer = CountVectorizer(stop_words='english')
X = vectorizer.fit_transform(documents)

# Apply LDA
lda = LatentDirichletAllocation(n_components=5, random_state=42)  # Set number of topics
lda.fit(X)

# Print topics
for index, topic in enumerate(lda.components_):
    print(f"Topic {index}:")
    print([vectorizer.get_feature_na ↓ _out()[i] for i in topic.argsort()[-10:]])
```

2.2. Non-Negative Matrix Factorization (NMF)

- **Overview:**
  - NMF is another method for topic modeling that is based on matrix factorization. It decomposes the term-document matrix into two lower-dimensional matrices: document-topic and topic- term matrices.

- **How It Works:**
  - **Matrix Factorization:** Decompose the term-document matrix into two non-negative matrices.

- **Iterative Optimization:** Use optimization algorithms to minimize the difference between the original matrix and the product of the two decomposed matrices.
- **Implementation:**

```
from sklearn.decomposition import NMF
from sklearn.feature_extraction.text import TfidfVectorizer

# Prepare the text data
vectorizer = TfidfVectorizer(stop_words='english')
X = vectorizer.fit_transform(documents)

# Apply NMF
nmf = NMF(n_components=5, random_state=42)  # Set number of topics
nmf.fit(X)

# Print topics
for index, topic in enumerate(nmf.components_):
    print(f"Topic {index}:")
    print([vectorizer.get_feature_names_out()[i] for i in topic.argsort()[-10:]])
```

2.3. Latent Semantic Analysis (LSA)

- **Overview:**
    - LSA is similar to LDA but is based on Singular Value Decomposition (SVD). It reduces the dimensionality of the term-document matrix to find the latent semantic structures.

- **How It Works:**
    - **SVD Decomposition:** Decompose the term-document matrix into three matrices using SVD.
    - **Dimensionality Reduction:** Retain a reduced number of singular values to approximate the original matrix.
    - **Implementation:**

```
from sklearn.decomposition import TruncatedSVD
from sklearn.feature_extraction.text import TfidfVectorizer

# Prepare the text data
vectorizer = TfidfVectorizer(stop_words='english')
X = vectorizer.fit_transform(documents)

# Apply LSA
lsa = TruncatedSVD(n_components=5, random_state=42)  # Set number of topics
lsa.fit(X)

# Print topics
for index, topic in enumerate(lsa.components_):
    print(f"Topic {index}:")
    print([vectorizer.get_feature_names_out()[i] for i in topic.argsort()[-10:]])
```

3. Evaluation and Interpretation

- **Topic Coherence:** Measures how semantically related the words in a topic are. High coherence scores indicate meaningful topics.
- **Human Interpretation:** Reviewing the top words of each topic to ensure they make sense and are interpretable.
- **Visualization Tools:** Tools like pyLDAvis can be used to visualize topics and their relationships.

4. Applications

- **Document Classification:** Classify documents into predefined topics.
- **Content Recommendation:** Suggest similar content based on the topic distribution.
- **Information Retrieval:** Improve search relevance by understanding the underlying topics of documents.

5. Limitations

- **Number of Topics:** The need to predefine the number of topics can be challenging and may require experimentation.
- **Interpretability:** Topics are based on probabilistic models, which may not always produce interpretable results.

Topic modeling is a powerful technique for uncovering the latent themes in large text corpora, helping in data exploration, summarization, and organization.

K-Means

K-Means is a popular clustering algorithm in machine learning that partitions a dataset into k clusters. Each cluster is defined by its centroid, which is the mean of the data points in that cluster. K-Means is widely used due to its simplicity and efficiency. Here's a detailed overview of the K-Means technique:

1. Concept of K-Means Clustering

- **Objective:** The goal of K-Means is to partition a set of observations into k clusters, where each observation belongs to the cluster with the nearest mean (centroid), minimizing the within-cluster variance.

2. How K-Means Works

1. **Initialization:**
   - **Choose k Initial Centroids:** Randomly select k data points from the dataset as the initial centroids. Alternatively, more sophisticated initialization methods like K-Means++ can be used to improve performance.

2. **Assignment Step:**
   - **Assign Data Points:** Assign each data point to the nearest centroid based on a distance metric, typically Euclidean distance. This forms k clusters.

3. **Update Step:**
   - **Recalculate Centroids:** Compute the mean of all data points assigned to each centroid to update the centroid's position.

4. **Repeat Steps:**
   - **Iterate:** Repeat the assignment and update steps until convergence, meaning the centroids no longer change, or the changes are below a specified threshold.

3. K-Means Algorithm in Python

Here's how you can implement K-Means clustering using Python and the scikit-learn library:

```
from sklearn.cluster import KMeans
from sklearn.preprocessing import StandardScaler
import numpy as np

# Sample data (replace with your own data)
data = np.array([
    [1, 2], [1, 4], [1, 0],
    [4, 2], [4, 4], [4, 0]
])

# Standardize the data (optional but recommended)
scaler = StandardScaler()
data_scaled = scaler.fit_transform(data)
```

```
# Apply K-Means
k = 2  # Number of clusters
kmeans = KMeans(n_clusters=k, random_state=42)
kmeans.fit(data_scaled)

# Get cluster assignments
labels = kmeans.labels_
print("Cluster assignments:", labels)

# Get cluster centroids
centroids = kmeans.cluster_centers_
print("Centroids:", centroids)
```

4. Choosing the Number of Clusters (k)

- **Elbow Method:**
  - Plot the sum of squared distances from each point to its assigned centroid (Within-Cluster Sum of Squares, or WCSS) for different values of k. The "elbow" point, where the rate of decrease sharply changes, suggests the optimal number of clusters.

```
import matplotlib.pyplot as plt

wcss = []
for i in range(1, 11):
    kmeans = KMeans(n_clusters=i, random_state=42)
    kmeans.fit(data_scaled)
    wcss.append(kmeans.inertia_)

plt.plot(range(1, 11), wcss)
plt.xlabel('Number of clusters')
plt.ylabel('WCSS')
plt.title('Elbow Method')
plt.show()
```

- **Silhouette Score:**
  - Measure how similar an object is to its own cluster compared to other clusters. The silhouette score ranges from -1 to 1, where a higher value indicates better-defined clusters.

```
from sklearn.metrics import silhouette_score

silhouette_avg = silhouette_score(data_scaled, labels)
print("Silhouette Score:", silhouette_avg)
```

5. Applications

- **Customer Segmentation:** Group customers based on purchasing behavior.
- **Image Compression:** Compress images by reducing the number of colors.
- **Anomaly Detection:** Identify outliers or anomalies by finding data points that do not fit well into any cluster.

6. Limitations

- **Number of Clusters (k):** The algorithm requires specifying the number of clusters in advance.
- **Cluster Shape:** K-Means assumes spherical clusters and may not work well with non-spherical or overlapping clusters.
- **Initialization Sensitivity:** Random initialization can lead to different results. K-Means++ improves initialization but doesn't eliminate the issue entirely.
- **Scalability:** K-Means can be sensitive to large datasets and outliers.

7. Advanced Variants

- **K-Means++:** Improves initialization by spreading out the initial centroids.
- **Mini-Batch K-Means:** A variant that uses mini-batches to speed up computation for large datasets.
- **Bisecting K-Means:** A hierarchical clustering approach that iteratively splits clusters.

K-Means is a fundamental and widely used clustering algorithm that, despite its simplicity, is very effective for many practical applications.

Linear regression

Linear regression is one of the most fundamental and widely used techniques in machine learning and statistics. It models the relationship between a dependent variable and one or more independent variables by fitting a linear equation to observed data. Here's a detailed overview of the linear regression technique:

1. Concept of Linear Regression

- **Objective:** To find the best-fitting linear relationship between the dependent variable (y) and the independent variables (X). This relationship is represented by a linear equation.
- **Equation:** For a simple linear regression (one independent variable), the model is:

y=β0+β1x+ϵy = \beta_0 + \beta_1 x + \epsilony=β0+β1x+ϵ Where:

- y is the dependent variable.
- x is the independent variable.
- β0\beta_0β0 is the intercept.
- β1\beta_1β1 is the slope or coefficient.
- ϵ\epsilonϵ is the error term.

For multiple linear regression (more than one independent variable), the model is:

y=β0+β1x1+β2x2+⋯+βnxn+ϵy = \beta_0 + \beta_1 x_1 + \beta_2 x_2 + \cdots + \beta_n x_n +\epsilony=β0+β1x1+β2x2+⋯+βnxn+ϵ

2.How Linear Regression Works

1. **Model Training:**
   - **Objective Function:** The goal is to minimize the cost function, which is typically the Mean Squared Error (MSE) between the predicted values and the actual values: MSE=1n∑i=1n(yi−y^i)2MSE = \frac{1}{n} \sum_{i=1}^n (y_i - \hat{y}_i)^2MSE=n1i=1∑n(yi−y^i)2 where y^i\hat{y}_iy^i is the predicted value for the i-th observation.
   - **Optimization:** Find the coefficients (weights) β0,β1,…,βn\beta_0, \beta_1, \ldots, \beta_nβ0,β1,…,βn that minimize the MSE. This is usually done using techniques like Ordinary Least Squares (OLS) or gradient descent.

2. Prediction:
   - Use the fitted model to predict the dependent variable for new data points:
   - y^=β0+β1x1+β2x2+⋯+βnxn\hat{y} = \beta_0 + \beta_1 x_1 + \beta_2 x_2 + \cdots + \beta_n x_ny^=β0+β1x1+β2x2+⋯+βnxn

3. Implementing Linear Regression in Python

You can use libraries like scikit-learn to easily implement

t linear regression. Here's a basic example:

```
from sklearn.linear_model import LinearRegression
from sklearn.model_selection import train_test_split
from sklearn.metrics import mean_squared_error
import numpy as np
```

```
# Sample data (replace with your own data)
X = np.array([[1], [2], [3], [4], [5]])  # Features
y = np.array([2, 3, 5, 7, 11])  # Target variable

# Split data into training and test sets
X_train, X_test, y_train, y_test = train_test_split(X, y, test_size=0.2, random_state=42)

# Create and fit the model
model = LinearRegression()
model.fit(X_train, y_train)

# Predict on test set
y_pred = model.predict(X_test)

# Evaluate the model
mse = mean_squared_error(y_test, y_pred)
print("Mean Squared Error:", mse)
print("Coefficients:", model.coef_)
print("Intercept:", model.intercept_)
```

4. Assumptions of Linear Regression

1. **Linearity:** The relationship between the dependent and independent variables is linear.
2. **Independence:** Observations are independent of each other.
3. **Homoscedasticity:** Constant variance of error terms.
4. **Normality:** The residuals (errors) of the model are normally distributed.

5. Applications

- **Predictive Modeling:** Forecasting sales, housing prices, etc.
- **Trend Analysis:** Identifying trends in time-series data.
- **Risk Assessment:** Evaluating risks and outcomes in finance and insurance.
- **Feature Importance:** Understanding the impact of different features on the target variable.

6. Limitations

- **Linearity Assumption:** Linear regression assumes a linear relationship, which might not always be true.

- **Outliers:** Sensitive to outliers, which can skew the results.
- **Multicollinearity:** When independent variables are highly correlated, it can lead to unreliable coefficient estimates.

7. Extensions and Variants

- **Polynomial Regression:** Extends linear regression by adding polynomial terms to the model to capture non-linear relationships.
- **Ridge Regression:** A variant that includes a regularization term to handle multicollinearity and prevent overfitting.
- **Lasso Regression:** Another variant with regularization that can also perform feature selection by shrinking some coefficients to zero.

Linear regression is a powerful technique that serves as the foundation for many more advanced machine learning methods. Understanding its principles and applications helps in effectively analyzing and predicting data.

Lasso Regression

Lasso Regression, or Least Absolute Shrinkage and Selection Operator, is a linear regression technique that incorporates L1 regularization to improve the model's performance and interpretability. By adding a penalty term to the linear regression model, Lasso Regression encourages sparsity in the model, effectively performing feature selection and regularization. Here's a detailed overview:

1. Concept of Lasso Regression

- **Objective:** Lasso Regression aims to minimize the residual sum of squares subject to a constraint on the sum of the absolute values of the coefficients. This constraint helps to prevent overfitting and promotes sparsity in the model.
- **Regularization Term:** The regularization term added to the linear regression cost function is the L1 norm of the coefficients:

$$\text{Cost Function} = \frac{1}{2n} \sum_{i=1}^{n} (y_i - \hat{y}_i)^2 + \lambda \sum_{j=1}^{p} |\beta_j|$$

Where:

- n is the number of observations.
- yi is the actual value for observation iii.
- y^i is the predicted value for observation iii.
- λ is the regularization parameter that controls the strength of the penalty.
- p is the number of predictors (features).
- βj represents the coefficients of the predictors.

Breakdown of the Cost Function:

1. **Mean Squared Error (MSE)**:

$\frac{1}{2n}\sum_{i=1}^{n}(y_i - \hat{y}_i)^2$ measures the average squared difference between the actual and predicted values, quantifying how well the model fits the data.

2. **L1 Regularization Term**:

$\lambda\sum_{j=1}^{p}|\beta_j|$ is the penalty term that encourages sparsity in the coefficients. The regularization parameter λ determines how much penalty is applied: larger values of λ increase the penalty, leading to more coefficients being shrunk to zero.

This formulation helps balance model accuracy with complexity, aiding in preventing overfitting while allowing for effective feature selection.

2. How Lasso Regression Works

1. **Model Training:**
   - **Objective Function:** Minimize the sum of the squared errors plus the regularization term.
   - **Regularization Parameter (λ):** Controls the strength of the regularization. Higher values of λ increase the penalty on the coefficients, leading to more shrinkage and sparser models.

2. **Feature Selection:**
   - Lasso Regression can shrink some coefficients to exactly zero, effectively performing feature selection by excluding less important features from the model.

3. Implementing Lasso Regression in Python

Using the scikit-learn library, you can easily implement Lasso Regression:

```
from sklearn.linear_model import Lasso
from sklearn.model_selection import train_test_split
from sklearn.metrics import mean_squared_error
import numpy as np
```

```
# Sample data (replace with your own data)
X = np.array([[1], [2], [3], [4], [5], [6], [7], [8], [9], [10]])  # Features
y = np.array([1.1, 2.2, 2.9, 4.1, 4.8, 6.0, 6.9, 8.2, 9.1, 10.1])  # Target variable

# Split data into training and test sets
X_train, X_test, y_train, y_test = train_test_split(X, y, test_size=0.2, random_state=42)

# Create and fit the Lasso model
alpha = 0.1  # Regularization parameter
lasso = Lasso(alpha=alpha)
lasso.fit(X_train, y_train)

# Predict on test set
y_pred = lasso.predict(X_test)

# Evaluate the model
mse = mean_squared_error(y_test, y_pred)
print("Mean Squared Error:", mse)
print("Coefficients:", lasso.coef_)
print("Intercept:", lasso.intercept_)
```

4. Choosing the Regularization Parameter (λ or α)

- **Cross-Validation:**
  - Use cross-validation to select the optimal regularization parameter that minimizes the error on the validation set.

```
from sklearn.linear_model import LassoCV

# Create LassoCV model to find optimal alpha
lasso_cv = LassoCV(alphas=np.logspace(-4, 4, 100), cv=5)
lasso_cv.fit(X_train, y_train)

print("Optimal alpha:", lasso_cv.alpha_)
```

5. Applications

- **Feature Selection:** By shrinking some coefficients to zero, Lasso helps in selecting important features, especially when dealing with high-dimensional data.
- **Regularization:** Reduces overfitting by penalizing large coefficients, making the model more generalizable.
- **Predictive Modeling:** Applied in various domains like finance, biology, and engineering to build interpretable models with reduced complexity.

6. Limitations

- **Bias-Variance Tradeoff:** While Lasso can improve generalization, excessive regularization may lead to underfitting.
- **Correlation Between Features:** When features are highly correlated, Lasso might randomly select one feature from the group and discard the others, which can lead to suboptimal models.

7. Extensions and Variants

- **Ridge Regression (L2 Regularization):** Uses L2 norm of the coefficients and tends to shrink coefficients but does not perform feature selection.
- **Elastic Net:** Combines L1 and L2 regularization, balancing between Lasso and Ridge Regression, and is useful when there are multiple correlated features.

Lasso Regression is a powerful tool for regularization and feature selection, particularly when dealing with high- dimensional datasets. By understanding and applying Lasso Regression, you can build more robust and interpretable machine learning models.

Ridge Regression

Ridge Regression, also known as L2 regularization, is a technique used in machine learning to enhance the performance and stability of linear regression models. It addresses some common problems associated with linear regression, such as multicollinearity and overfitting, by adding a penalty to the model's complexity. Here's a detailed look at Ridge Regression (L2 regularization), including its mechanics, implementation, and applications:

1. Concept and Purpose

Addressing Multicollinearity:

- **Problem:** Multicollinearity occurs when predictor variables are highly correlated, making it challenging to estimate the regression coefficients accurately.
- **Solution:** Ridge Regression helps by adding a regularization term, which stabilizes the coefficient estimates.

Preventing Overfitting:

- **Problem:** Overfitting happens when a model learns the noise in the training data instead of the underlying pattern, leading to poor generalization.

- **Solution:** The regularization term in Ridge Regression shrinks the coefficients, reducing model complexity and improving generalization.

Regularization Term:

- **Objective:** The regularization term penalizes large coefficients, discouraging the model from fitting the noise in the data.
- **Formula:** The Ridge Regression loss function includes a penalty term:

$$\text{Loss} = \text{RSS} + \lambda \sum_{j=1}^{p} \beta_j^2$$

Where:

- **RSS (Residual Sum of Squares):** Measures the discrepancy between the observed and predicted values.

$$\text{RSS} = \sum_{i=1}^{n} (y_i - \hat{y}_i)^2$$

- **λ:** Regularization parameter that controls the strength of the penalty.
- **βj:** Coefficients of the features.

2. How Ridge Regression Works

Objective Function:

- Ridge Regression modifies the ordinary least squares (OLS) objective function by adding the L2 regularization term:

$$\text{Objective} = \|X\beta - y\|^2 + \lambda\|\beta\|^2$$

Where:

- **X:** Feature matrix.
- **β:** Coefficient vector.
- **y:** Target vector.
- **λ∥β∥2\lambda \| \beta \|^2λ∥β∥2:** Regularization term.

Closed-Form Solution:

- Ridge regression provides a closed-form solution for the coefficient estimates, which can be derived from the objective function. The closed-form solution is given by:

$$\hat{\beta} = (X^T X + \lambda I)^{-1} X^T y$$

Where:

- **I:** Identity matrix.
- **(XTX+λI)(X^T X + \lambda I)(XTX+λI) is invertible**, ensuring a stable solution even when multicollinearity is present.

3. Implementation

```
from sklearn.linear_model import Ridge
from sklearn.preprocessing import StandardScaler

# Assuming X is the feature matrix and y is the target vector
scaler = StandardScaler()
X_scaled = scaler.fit_transform(X)

# Initialize and fit Ridge Regression model
ridge = Ridge(alpha=1.0)  # alpha is the regularization parameter (λ)
ridge.fit(X_scaled, y)

# Predict and access coefficients
predictions = ridge.predict(X_scaled)
coefficients = ridge.coef_
```

4. Choosing the Regularization Parameter (λ)

Cross-Validation:

- **Objective:** Select the optimal λ\lambdaλ value that minimizes prediction error.
- **Method:** Use k-fold cross-validation to evaluate different λ\lambdaλ values and select the one that performs best.

Grid Search:

- **Objective:** Perform an exhaustive search over a predefined range of λ\lambdaλ values to find the best parameter.

5. Applications

Handling Multicollinearity:

- Ridge Regression stabilizes coefficient estimates when predictor variables are highly correlated.

Improving Model Performance:

- By shrinking coefficients, Ridge Regression can enhance

generalization and prevent overfitting, especially in high-dimensional datasets.

Feature Scaling:

- Ridge Regression requires feature scaling to ensure all features contribute equally to the regularization term. Standardize features before applying the model.

6. Limitations

No Feature Elimination:

- Ridge Regression does not set any coefficients to zero, so it does not perform feature selection. Unlike Lasso Regression, it does not produce sparse solutions.

Interpretability:

- The coefficients are shrunk but not eliminated, which can make interpretation challenging compared to models that perform explicit feature selection.

Linearity:

- Ridge Regression assumes linear relationships between features and the target variable. It may not be suitable for non-linear relationships unless combined with non-linear transformations.

7. Summary

Ridge Regression (L2 regularization) is a valuable technique for improving the stability and generalization of linear regression models. By adding a penalty for large coefficients, Ridge Regression addresses multicollinearity and overfitting, particularly in high-dimensional settings. Understanding and applying Ridge Regression can help enhance the performance of your machine-learning models and manage complex datasets more effectively.

Logistic Regression

Logistic Regression is a widely used classification technique in machine learning that is particularly effective for binary classification problems but can be extended to multi-class problems as well. Despite its name, logistic regression is used for classification rather than regression. Here's a detailed overview of Logistic Regression:

1. Concept and Purpose

Classification Problem:

- **Objective:** Logistic Regression predicts the probability that a given input belongs to a particular class. It is used for binary classification (e.g., spam vs. non-spam) and can be extended to multiclass classification.

Logistic Function:

- **Sigmoid Function:** Logistic Regression uses the logistic (sigmoid) function to model the probability that a given input belongs to the positive class. The sigmoid function maps any real-valued number into the range [0, 1], making it suitable for binary classification:

$$\sigma(z) = \frac{1}{1 + e^{-z}}$$

Where z is the linear combination of features.

2. How Logistic Regression Works

Model Representation:

- Logistic Regression models the probability of the positive class using a linear combination of input features:

$$P(y = 1|X) = \sigma(X\beta)$$

Where:

- **X** is the feature matrix.
- **β** is the vector of coefficients.
- **σ** is the sigmoid function.

Decision Boundary:

- The decision boundary is the threshold at which the model predicts class membership. For binary classification, this is typically set at 0.5. If the predicted probability P(y=1|X)P(y = 1 | X)P(y=1|X) is greater than 0.5, the observation is classified as class 1; otherwise, it is classified as class 0.

Objective Function:

- The goal is to maximize the likelihood of the observed data given the model parameters. This is achieved by minimizing the negative log-likelihood (or equivalently, maximizing the log-likelihood):

$$\text{Log-Likelihood} = \sum_{i=1}^{n} \left[y_i \log(\hat{p}_i) + (1 - y_i) \log(1 - \hat{p}_i) \right]$$

Where:

- **yi**: This is the actual outcome for the i-th observation, where yi is either 0 or 1.
- **p^i** : is the predicted probability for the i-th observation.

$$\hat{p}_i = \sigma(X_i\beta) = \frac{1}{1 + e^{-(X_i\beta)}}$$

Where Xi is the feature vector for the i-th observation.

3. Implementation

Python (scikit-learn):

```
from sklearn.linear_model import LogisticRegression
from sklearn.preprocessing import StandardScaler
```

```
from sklearn.model_selection import train_test_split
from sklearn.metrics import accuracy_score, confusion_matrix, classification_report

# Sample data
X = ...  # Feature matrix
y = ...  # Target vector

# Split the data
X_train, X_test, y_train, y_test = train_test_split(X, y, test_size=0.3, random_state=42)

# Standardize the data
scaler = StandardScaler()
X_train_scaled = scaler.fit_transform(X_train)
X_test_scaled = scaler.transform(X_test)

# Initialize and fit Logistic Regression model
model = LogisticRegression()
model.fit(X_train_scaled, y_train)

# Predict and evaluate
predictions = model.predict(X_test_scaled)
accuracy = accuracy_score(y_test, predictions)
conf_matrix = confusion_matrix(y_test, predictions)
class_report = classification_report(y_test, predictions)

print(f"Accuracy: {accuracy}")
print(f"Confusion Matrix:\n{conf_matrix}")
print(f"Classification Report:\n{class_report}")
```

4. Interpreting Results

Coefficients:

- The coefficients (β) represent the change in the log odds of the dependent variable for a one-unit change in the predictor variable, holding other variables constant.

Probability Threshold:

- The default threshold is 0.5. Adjusting the threshold can affect precision and recall. For example, lowering the threshold may increase recall but decrease precision.

Confusion Matrix:

- A confusion matrix provides a summary of prediction results, including true positives, false positives, true negatives, and false negatives.

Classification Report:

- Includes metrics such as precision, recall, F1-score, and support for each class.

5. Applications

Binary Classification:

- Commonly used for problems with two possible outcomes (e.g., email spam detection, disease diagnosis).

Multiclass Classification:

- Can be extended to handle multiple classes using techniques like one-vs-rest or softmax regression.

Probability Estimates:

- Provides probability estimates for class membership, which can be useful for risk assessment and decision-making.

6. Limitations

Linearity:

- Assumes a linear relationship between features and the log-odds of the outcome. It may not perform well with non-linear relationships unless combined with non-linear transformations.

Outliers:

- Logistic Regression can be sensitive to outliers, which may affect model performance.

Interpretability:

- While coefficients are interpretable, the model may become complex with many features, especially in high-dimensional spaces.

7. Summary

Logistic Regression is a powerful and interpretable classification technique used for binary and multiclass classification problems. By modeling the probability of a given class using a logistic function provides insights into the relationships between features and the target variable. Understanding and applying Logistic Regression effectively can enhance the performance of classification tasks and provide meaningful insights from data.

Linear Discriminant Analysis (LDA)

Linear Discriminant Analysis (LDA) is a powerful technique used in machine learning for dimensionality reduction and classification. It focuses on finding a linear combination of features that best separates two or more classes of objects or events. Here's an in-depth look at LDA, including its concept, workings, implementation, and applications:

1. Concept and Purpose

Dimensionality Reduction:

- **Objective:** Reduce the number of features while retaining the most discriminatory information between classes.
- **Benefit:** Simplifies models, reduces computational costs, and mitigates the risk of overfitting by focusing on the most informative features.

Classification:

- **Objective:** Use the linear combinations of features to classify observations into different classes.
- **Benefit:** Provides a clear decision boundary by maximizing class separability.

Class Separation:

- **LDA seeks to maximize the distance between the means of different classes while minimizing the variance within each class.**

2. How LDA Works

1. **Compute the Mean Vectors:**

- For each class, compute the mean vector μk\mu kμk of the features.

2. Compute the Within-Class Scatter Matrix:

- Measures the scatter (variance) of features within each class:

Where:

$$S_W = \sum_{k=1}^{K} \sum_{x_i \in C_k} (x_i - \mu_k)(x_i - \mu_k)^T$$

- **K** is the number of classes.
- **Ck** is the set of data points in class k.
- **μk** is the mean vector of class k.

3. Compute the Between-Class Scatter Matrix:

- Measures the scatter between different class means:

$$S_B = \sum_{k=1}^{K} n_k(\mu_k - \mu)(\mu_k - \mu)^T$$

Where:

- **nk** is the number of samples in class kkk.
- **μ** is the overall mean of all data points.

4. Compute the Eigenvalues and Eigenvectors:

- Solve the generalized eigenvalue problem for the matrix

$$S_W^{-1} S_B \cdot v = \lambda \cdot v$$

Where:

- **λ** represents the eigenvalues.
- **v** represents the eigenvectors (discriminant vectors).

5. Select the Top Eigenvectors:

- Choose the eigenvectors corresponding to the largest eigenvalues. These eigenvectors form the new feature space (discriminants).

6. Transform Data:

- Project the original data onto the new feature space using the selected eigenvectors.

$$X_{lda} = X \cdot W$$

Where **W** is the matrix of selected eigenvectors.

X: This is the original data matrix, where each row represents an observation and each column represents a feature.

$$S_W^{-1} S_B \cdot v = \lambda \cdot v.$$

W: This is the matrix of selected eigenvectors obtained from the generalized eigenvalue problem. Each column of W corresponds to an eigenvector associated with the largest eigenvalues, indicating the directions that maximize class separability.

Xlda: This is the projected data matrix in the new feature space. Each observation is represented in terms of the new axes defined by the eigenvectors in W.

3. Implementation in Python

Python (scikit-learn):

```
from sklearn.discriminant_analysis import LinearDiscriminantAnalysis
from sklearn.preprocessing import StandardScaler
from sklearn.model_selection import train_test_split
from sklearn.metrics import accuracy_score, confusion_matrix, classification_report
import numpy as np

# Sample data (replace with actual data)
X = np.random.rand(100, 5)  # Feature matrix with 100 samples and 5 features
y = np.random.randint(0, 3, 100)  # Target vector with 3 classes

# Split the data
X_train, X_test, y_train, y_test = train_test_split(X, y, test_size=0.3, random_state=42)

# Standardize the data
scaler = StandardScaler()
X_train_scaled = scaler.fit_transform(X_train)
X_test_scaled = scaler.transform(X_test)

# Initialize and fit LDA model
lda = LinearDiscriminantAnalysis()
lda.fit(X_train_scaled, y_train)

# Transform data
X_train_lda = lda.transform(X_train_scaled)
X_test_lda = lda.transform(X_test_scaled)
```

```
# Predict and evaluate
predictions = lda.predict(X_test_lda)
accuracy = accuracy_score(y_test, predictions)
conf_matrix = confusion_matrix(y_test, predictions)
class_report = classification_report(y_test, predictions)

print(f"Accuracy: {accuracy}")
print(f"Confusion Matrix:\n{conf_matrix}")
print(f"Classification Report:\n{class_report}")
```

4. Applications

Dimensionality Reduction:

- **Objective:** Reduce the number of features while retaining the most important discriminatory information.
- **Benefit:** Simplifies models and improves interpretability

Classification:

- **Objective:** Use the reduced feature space to classify observations into different classes.
- **Benefit:** Provides a clear and interpretable decision boundary.

Face Recognition and Image Classification:

- **Objective:** Identify individuals or classify images based on reduced feature space.
- **Benefit:** Efficiently handles high-dimensional image data.

5. Advantages

- **Simplicity and Efficiency:**
  - LDA is computationally efficient and relatively simple compared to other classification methods.
- **Interpretability:**
  - Provides clear insights into which features contribute most to class separability.

- **Handles Multiclass Problems:**
    - Extends naturally to problems with more than two classes.

6. Limitations

- **Assumption of Linearity:**
    - Assumes that the relationship between features and the log-odds of class membership is linear. May not perform well with non-linear relationships.
- **Assumption of Normality:**
    - Assumes that features within each class are normally distributed. Deviations from this assumption can affect performance.
- **Sensitivity to Outliers:**
    - Sensitive to outliers, which can impact the estimation of class means and covariance matrices.

7. Summary

Linear Discriminant Analysis (LDA) is a valuable technique for both dimensionality reduction and classification. By focusing on maximizing class separability, LDA simplifies the model and enhances its interpretability.

Understanding and applying LDA effectively can improve the performance of classification tasks, particularly in high-dimensional data scenarios.

Quadratic Discriminant Analysis (QDA)

Quadratic Discriminant Analysis (QDA) is a classification technique used in machine learning that extends the idea of Linear Discriminant Analysis (LDA) by allowing for a more flexible decision boundary between classes. Unlike LDA, which assumes that classes share the same covariance matrix and thus produce linear decision boundaries, QDA allows each class to have its own covariance matrix, resulting in quadratic decision boundaries.

1. Concept and Purpose

Quadratic Discriminant Analysis (QDA):

- **Objective**: Classify data points by finding decision boundaries that are quadratic functions of the features.
- **Benefit**: Provides a more flexible decision boundary compared to LDA, which can be advantageous when the classes are not linearly separable.

2. How QDA Works

QDA is based on the assumption that features within each class are normally distributed. It estimates the parameters of these distributions for each class and then uses them to classify new data points.

1. **Compute the Mean Vectors:**
   - For each class k, compute the mean vector μk of the features.
   - Formula:

$$\mu_k = \frac{1}{n_k} \sum_{x_i \in C_k} x_i$$

, where nk is the number of samples in class k, and Ck is the set of data points in class k.

2. **Compute the Covariance Matrices:**
   - Each class k has its own covariance matrix.
   - Formula:

$$\Sigma_k = \frac{1}{n_k - 1} \sum_{x_i \in C_k} (x_i - \mu_k)(x_i - \mu_k)^T$$

3. Compute the Prior Probabilities:
   - Compute the prior probability for each class, which is the proportion of data points belonging to that class.
   - Formula:

$$\pi_k = \frac{n_k}{N}$$

, where N is the total number of data points.

4. Classify New Data Points:
   - To classify a new data point x, compute the posterior probability for each class and assign the point to the class with the highest posterior probability.
   - The posterior probability is computed using Bayes' theorem:

$$P(C_k|x) \propto \pi_k \cdot \frac{1}{(2\pi)^{d/2}|\Sigma_k|^{1/2}} \exp\left(-\frac{1}{2}(x - \mu_k)^T \Sigma_k^{-1} (x - \mu_k)\right)$$

- Here, d is the number of features, and $|\Sigma k|$ is the determinant of the covariance matrix Σk.

3. Implementation in Python

Here's how you can implement QDA in Python using the scikit-learn library:

Python

```
from sklearn.discriminant_analysis import QuadraticDiscriminantAnalysis
from sklearn.preprocessing import StandardScaler
from sklearn.model_selection import train_test_split
from sklearn.metrics import accuracy_score, confusion_matrix, classification_report
import numpy as np

# Sample data (replace with actual data)
X = np.random.rand(100, 5)  # Feature matrix with 100 samples and 5 features
y = np.random.randint(0, 3, 100)  # Target vector with 3 classes

# Split the data
X_train, X_test, y_train, y_test = train_test_split(X, y, test_size=0.3, random_state=42)

# Standardize the data
scaler = StandardScaler()
X_train_scaled = scaler.fit_transform(X_train)
X_test_scaled = scaler.transform(X_test)

# Initialize and fit QDA model
qda = QuadraticDiscriminantAnalysis()
qda.fit(X_train_scaled, y_train)

# Predict and evaluate
predictions = qda.predict(X_test_scaled)
accuracy = accuracy_score(y_test, predictions)
conf_matrix = confusion_matrix(y_test, predictions)
class_report = classification_report(y_test, predictions)


print(f"Accuracy: {accuracy}")
print(f"Confusion Matrix:\n{conf_matrix}")
print(f"Classification Report:\n{class_report}")
```

4. Applications

Classification:

- QDA is used for classification tasks where the relationship between features and class labels is expected to be nonlinear.

Financial Modeling:

- Can be applied to classify financial assets or credit risk, where the covariance structure of different asset returns may differ significantly.

Medical Diagnosis:

- Useful in medical applications where different classes (e.g., disease vs. no disease) may have different variances in feature measurements.

5. Advantages

- **Flexibility in Decision Boundaries:**
    - QDA allows for quadratic decision boundaries, which can capture more complex relationships between features and class labels.

- **Handles Different Covariance Structures:**
    - Unlike LDA, QDA does not assume that all classes share the same covariance matrix, making it more flexible in modeling real-world data.

6. Limitations

- **Computational Complexity:**
    - QDA requires the computation of a separate covariance matrix for each class, which can be computationally expensive, especially in high-dimensional spaces.
- **Assumption of Normality:**
    - Assumes that features are normally distributed within each class. Deviations from this assumption can affect performance.

- **Sensitivity to Small Sample Sizes:**
    - With small sample sizes, covariance matrix estimates can be unstable, which might lead to poor classification performance.

7. Summary

Quadratic Discriminant Analysis (QDA) extends Linear Discriminant Analysis by allowing for quadratic decision boundaries. This provides a more flexible approach to classification when classes have different covariance structures. While QDA can capture more complex relationships than LDA, it also comes with increased computational complexity and sensitivity to deviations from normality. Understanding these trade-offs is crucial for effectively applying QDA to real-world problems.

K-Nearest Neighbors (KNN)

K-Nearest Neighbors (KNN) is a simple yet powerful machine learning algorithm used for classification and regression tasks. It's based on the idea that similar data points are close to each other in feature space. KNN is known for its simplicity and effectiveness in various scenarios.

1. Concept and Purpose

K-Nearest Neighbors (KNN):

- **Objective**: Classify data points or predict values based on the nearest neighbors in the feature space.
- **Benefit**: Intuitive and straightforward, KNN is effective for problems where the decision boundary is not linear and can be adapted to both classification and regression tasks.

2. How KNN Works

Classification:

1. **Choose the Number of Neighbors (k)**:
    - Select a positive integer k that determines how many nearest neighbors will be considered for classifying a new data point.

1. **Calculate Distances:**
   - Compute the distance between the new data point and all other data points in the training set. Common distance metrics include Euclidean distance, Manhattan distance, and Minkowski distance.
2. **Identify Nearest Neighbors:**
   - Identify the k nearest neighbors to the new data point based on the calculated distances.
3. **Vote for Class Labels:**
   - For classification, the new data point is assigned the most common class label among its k nearest neighbors. If k=5k = 5k=5, for example, the majority class among the five nearest neighbors determines the class of the new point.

Regression:

1. **Choose the Number of Neighbors (k):**
   - Select a positive integer k for the number of nearest neighbors.
2. **Calculate Distances:**
   - Compute the distance between the new data point and all other data points in the training set.
3. **Identify Nearest Neighbors:**
   - Identify the k nearest neighbors.
4. **Predict the Target Value:**
   - For regression, the prediction for the new data point is typically the average (or weighted average) of the target values of its k nearest neighbors.

3. Implementation in Python

Here's how you can implement KNN using the scikit-learn library for both classification and regression:

Classification Example:

Python

```
from sklearn.neighbors import KNeighborsClassifier
from sklearn.preprocessing import StandardScaler
from sklearn.model_selection import train_test_split
from sklearn.metrics import accuracy_score, confusion_matrix, classification_report
import numpy as np

# Sample data (replace with actual data)
X = np.random.rand(100, 5)  # Feature matrix with 100 samples and 5 features
y = np.random.randint(0, 3, 100)  # Target vector with 3 classes

# Split the data
X_train, X_test, y_train, y_test = train_test_split(X, y, test_size=0.3, random_state=42)

# Standardize the data
scaler = StandardScaler()
X_train_scaled = scaler.fit_transform(X_train)
X_test_scaled = scaler.transform(X_test)
# Initialize and fit KNN model
knn = KNeighborsClassifier(n_neighbors=5)  # Use k=5 for this example
knn.fit(X_train_scaled, y_train)

# Predict and evaluate
predictions = knn.predict(X_test_scaled)
accuracy = accuracy_score(y_test, predictions)
conf_matrix = confusion_matrix(y_test, predictions)
class_report = classification_report(y_test, predictions)

print(f"Accuracy: {accuracy}")
print(f"Confusion Matrix:\n{conf_matrix}")
print(f"Classification Report:\n{class_report}")
```

Regression Example:

Python

```
from sklearn.neighbors import KNeighborsRegressor
from sklearn.preprocessing import StandardScaler
from sklearn.model_selection import train_test_split
from sklearn.metrics import mean_squared_error, r2_score
import numpy as np

# Sample data (replace with actual data)
X = np.random.rand(100, 5)  # Feature matrix with 100 samples and 5 features
y = np.random.rand(100)  # Continuous target vector
```

4. Applications

Classification:

- **Spam Detection:** Classifying emails as spam or not spam.
- **Image Recognition:** Classifying images into categories based on pixel features.
- **Medical Diagnosis:** Classifying patient data into disease categories.

Regression:

- **Predicting House Prices:** Estimating house prices based on features like size, location, and number of rooms.
- **Stock Price Prediction:** Forecasting stock prices based on historical data.

5. Advantages

1. **Simplicity:**
    - KNN is easy to understand and implement, requiring no training phase as it is a lazy learner.
2. **No Assumptions about Data Distribution:**
    - KNN does not make any assumptions about the underlying data distribution, which is beneficial for datasets where relationships between features are complex.

3. **Adaptability:**
    - Can be used for both classification and regression tasks.

6. Limitations

1. **Computational Complexity:**
    - KNN can be computationally expensive during prediction, as it requires calculating distances to all training samples.
2. **Memory Usage:**
    - Requires storing the entire training dataset, which can be a drawback for large datasets.
3. **Sensitive to Feature Scaling:**
    - The performance of KNN can be significantly affected by the scale of features, so feature scaling is important.
4. **Choice of k:**
    - The choice of k can significantly impact performance. A small k might lead to noisy predictions, while a large k might smooth out the predictions too much.
5. **Curse of Dimensionality:**
    - As the number of features increases, the distance between points becomes less meaningful, which can degrade performance. Feature selection or dimensionality reduction techniques may be needed.

7. Summary

K-Nearest Neighbors (KNN) is a versatile algorithm used for both classification and regression tasks. It classifies or predicts new data points based on the labels or values of the nearest training samples. While KNN is simple and intuitive, it can be computationally expensive and sensitive to feature scaling and the choice of k. Proper preprocessing and tuning are essential for achieving optimal performance with KNN.

Neural Networks (NNs)

Neural Networks (NNs) are a fundamental technique in machine learning and artificial intelligence inspired by the structure and function of the human brain. They are particularly powerful for modeling complex patterns and relationships in data and can be used for a wide range of tasks, including classification, regression, and more.

1. Concept and Purpose

Neural Networks (NNs):

- **Objective**: Model complex relationships between inputs and outputs by learning from data through interconnected layers of nodes (neurons).
- **Benefit**: Capable of capturing intricate patterns and features in data, making them effective for tasks like image recognition, natural language processing, and time-series prediction.

2. Structure of Neural Networks

1. **Neurons and Layers:**
    - **Neurons**: Basic units that receive inputs, apply weights, and pass through an activation function to produce an output.

- **Layers:**
  - **Input Layer**: Receives the raw input features.
  - **Hidden Layers**: Intermediate layers between input and output, where computations and feature transformations occur. Each hidden layer consists of multiple neurons.
  - **Output Layer**: Produces the final prediction or output of the network.

1. **Activation Functions:**
   - **Purpose**: Introduce non-linearity into the network, allowing it to learn and model complex functions.
   - **Common Functions:**
     - **Sigmoid**:

$$\sigma(x) = \frac{1}{1 + e^{-x}}$$

     - **ReLU (Rectified Linear Unit)**: ReLU(x)=max(0,x)
     - **Tanh**:

$$\tanh(x) = \frac{e^x - e^{-x}}{e^x + e^{-x}}$$

     - **Softmax**: Converts logits to probabilities in classification problems.
2. **Learning Process:**
   - **Forward Propagation**: Pass input data through the network to get predictions.
   - **Loss Function**: Measures the difference between predicted and actual values. Common loss functions include Mean Squared Error (MSE) for regression and Cross-Entropy Loss for classification.
   - **Backpropagation**: Updates the weights of the network by computing gradients of the loss function with respect to each weight using techniques like gradient descent.

3. Implementation in Python

Neural Networks are commonly implemented using libraries such as TensorFlow and PyTorch. Here's a simple

example using scikit-learn, which includes a basic neural network model:

Classification Example:

Python

```
from sklearn.neural_network import MLPClassifier
from sklearn.preprocessing import StandardScaler
from sklearn.model_selection import train_test_split
from sklearn.metrics import accuracy_score, confusion_matrix, classification_report
import numpy as np

# Sample data (replace with actual data)
X = np.random.rand(100, 5)  # Feature matrix with 100 samples and 5 features
y = np.random.randint(0, 3, 100)  # Target vector with 3 classes

# Split the data
X_train, X_test, y_train, y_test = train_test_split(X, y, test_size=0.3, random_state=42)

# Standardize the data
scaler = StandardScaler()
X_train_scaled = scaler.fit_transform(X_train)
X_test_scaled = scaler.transform(X_test)

# Initialize and fit Neural Network model
mlp = MLPClassifier(hidden_layer_sizes=(10, 5), max_iter=1000, random_state=42)
mlp.fit(X_train_scaled, y_train)

# Predict and evaluate
predictions = mlp.predict(X_test_scaled)
accuracy = accuracy_score(y_test, predictions)
conf_matrix = confusion_matrix(y_test, predictions)
class_report = classification_report(y_test, predictions)

print(f"Accuracy: {accuracy}")
print(f"Confusion Matrix:\n{conf_matrix}")
print(f"Classification Report:\n{class_report}")
```

Regression Example:

Python

```
from sklearn.neural_network import MLPRegressor
from sklearn.preprocessing import StandardScaler
from sklearn.model_selection import train_test_split
from sklearn.metrics import mean_squared_error, r2_score
import numpy as np

# Sample data (replace with actual data)
X = np.random.rand(100, 5)  # Feature matrix with 100 samples and 5 features
y = np.random.rand(100)  # Continuous target vector
```

```
# Split the data
X_train, X_test, y_train, y_test = train_test_split(X, y, test_size=0.3, random_state=42)
# Standardize the data
scaler = StandardScaler()
X_train_scaled = scaler.fit_transform(X_train)
X_test_scaled = scaler.transform(X_test)

# Initialize and fit Neural Network model
mlp = MLPRegressor(hidden_layer_sizes=(10, 5), max_iter=1000, random_state=42)
mlp.fit(X_train_scaled, y_train)

# Predict and evaluate
predictions = mlp.predict(X_test_scaled)
mse = mean_squared_error(y_test, predictions)
r2 = r2_score(y_test, predictions)

print(f"Mean Squared Error: {mse}")
print(f"R^2 Score: {r2}")
```

4. Applications

Classification:

- **Image Recognition:** Classify objects in images (e.g., identifying faces or animals).
- **Spam Detection:** Classify emails as spam or not spam.
- **Medical Diagnosis:** Predict diseases based on patient data.

Regression:

- **House Price Prediction:** Estimate property prices based on features like size and location.
    - **Stock Market Prediction:** Forecast future stock prices based on historical data.

Advantages

- **Flexibility and Power:**
    - Neural Networks can model complex and non-linear relationships, making them suitable for a wide range of applications.
- **Feature Learning:**
    - They can automatically learn and extract features from raw data, reducing the need for manual feature engineering.
- **Scalability:**
    - Neural Networks can scale with data and complexity, allowing for deep learning with many layers and large datasets.

6. Limitations

- **Computationally Intensive:**
    - Training deep neural networks can be computationally expensive and time-consuming, often requiring specialized hardware like GPUs.
- **Require Large Datasets:**
    - They typically perform better with large amounts of data. Small datasets might lead to overfitting.

- **Interpretability:**
  - Neural Networks are often considered "black boxes" because their internal workings are not
    - easily interpretable, making it challenging to understand how they make decisions.
- **Hyperparameter Tuning:**
  - Selecting the right architecture, activation functions, and other hyperparameters can be complex and require experimentation.

7. Summary

Neural Networks are a versatile and powerful machine learning technique capable of solving various problems in classification, regression, and more. They excel at modeling complex patterns and relationships in data. However, they also come with challenges, such as computational requirements, the need for large datasets, and difficulties in interpretability. Understanding and addressing these challenges is crucial for effectively applying neural networks to real-world problems.

Reinforcement Learning (RL)

Reinforcement Learning (RL) is a type of machine learning where an agent learns to make decisions by performing actions and receiving feedback from the environment. Unlike supervised learning, where models are trained on labeled data, RL involves learning through trial and error to maximize cumulative rewards.

1. Concept and Purpose

Reinforcement Learning (RL):

- **Objective**: Train an agent to make a sequence of decisions to maximize cumulative rewards over time.
- **Benefit**: Useful for problems where the correct actions are not explicitly known and must be discovered through interaction with the environment.

2. Key Components of RL

1. **Agent**: The entity that learns and makes decisions. It interacts with the environment to achieve its goals.
2. **Environment**: The external system with which the agent interacts. It provides feedback and rewards based on the agent's actions.

3. **State**: A representation of the current situation of the environment. The state helps the agent decide what actions to take.
4. **Action**: The choices or moves that the agent can make. Actions affect the state of the environment and are selected based on the current state.
5. **Reward**: Feedback received from the environment after taking an action. Rewards indicate how good orbad the action was in terms of achieving the agent's goal.
6. **Policy**: A strategy the agent uses to decide which action to take in a given state. It can be deterministic (fixed action for each state) or stochastic (probabilistic action choices).
7. **Value Function**: A function that estimates the expected cumulative reward that can be obtained from a state or state-action pair. It helps the agent evaluate the desirability of states or actions.
8. **Q-Function (Action-Value Function)**: Estimates the expected cumulative reward for taking a specific action in a given state and following the policy thereafter.

3. Key Concepts and Algorithms

- **Exploration vs. Exploitation:**
  - **Exploration**: Trying new actions to discover their effects.
  - **Exploitation**: Using known actions that yield the highest reward based on past experience.
- **Markov Decision Process (MDP):**
  - A mathematical framework used to describe an RL problem. It consists of states, actions, rewards, and transitions between states.
- **Bellman Equation:**
  - Provides a recursive decomposition for the value function. This helps us understand how the value of a state or action can be computed based on the values of subsequent states or actions.
- **Dynamic Programming:**
  - Techniques used to solve RL problems include systematically breaking down problems into simpler subproblems. Examples include Value Iteration and Policy Iteration.

- **Temporal Difference (TD) Learning:**
  - Combines ideas from Monte Carlo methods and dynamic programming. TD methods update value estimates based on other learned estimates without waiting for a final outcome. Examples include Q-learning and SARSA.
- **Deep Reinforcement Learning:**
  - Combines RL with deep learning techniques to handle high-dimensional state spaces and complex environments. Deep Q-Networks (DQN) and Deep Deterministic Policy Gradient (DDPG) are popular algorithms in this area.

4. Implementation in Python

Using the Gym library for environments and Stable Baselines3 for RL algorithms:

Example: Q-Learning with Gym

python

```
import gym
import numpy as np

# Initialize environment
env = gym.make('Taxi-v3')

# Q-Table Initialization
n_actions = env.action_space.n
n_states = env.observation_space.n
Q = np.zeros((n_states, n_actions))

# Parameters
alpha = 0.1  # Learning rate
gamma = 0.9  # Discount factor
epsilon = 0.1  # Exploration rate
n_episodes = 1000

# Q-Learning Algorithm
for episode in range(n_episodes):
    state = env.reset()
    done = False
    while not done:
        if np.random.rand() < epsilon:
            action = env.action_space.sample()  # Explore
        else:
            action = np.argmax(Q[state])  # Exploit

        next_state, reward, done, _ = env.step(action)

        # Q-Update
        Q[state, action] += alpha * (reward + gamma * np.max(Q[next_state]) - Q[state, action])

        state = next_state

print("Training complete.")
```

Example: Using Stable Baselines3

python

```python
import gym
import numpy as np

# Initialize environment
env = gym.make('Taxi-v3')

# Q-Table Initialization
n_actions = env.action_space.n
n_states = env.observation_space.n
Q = np.zeros((n_states, n_actions))

# Parameters
alpha = 0.1  # Learning rate
gamma = 0.9  # Discount factor
epsilon = 0.1  # Exploration rate
n_episodes = 1000

# Q-Learning Algorithm
for episode in range(n_episodes):
    state = env.reset()
    done = False
    while not done:
        if np.random.rand() < epsilon:
            action = env.action_space.sample()  # Explore
        else:
            action = np.argmax(Q[state])  # Exploit

        next_state, reward, done, _ = env.step(action)

        # Q-Update
        Q[state, action] += alpha * (reward + gamma * np.max(Q[next_state]) - Q[state, action])

        state = next_state

print("Training complete.")
```

5. Applications

- **Game Playing:**
  - RL has been successfully applied to games like Chess, Go, and various video games, where the agent learns to play and improve performance through self-play.
- **Robotics:**
  - Used for training robots to perform tasks like walking, grasping objects, and navigation in complex environments.
- **Autonomous Vehicles:**
  - Applied in training self-driving cars to make driving decisions based on sensor data and environmental conditions.
- **Finance:**
  - Employed in algorithmic trading and portfolio management to make decisions based on market data and reward structures.
- **Healthcare:**
  - Utilized for personalized treatment planning and optimizing resource allocation in healthcare settings.

6. Advantages

- **Adaptability:**
  - Can handle dynamic and complex environments where the optimal actions are unknown beforehand.
- **Ability to Learn from Interaction:**
  - Learns optimal strategies through interactions and feedback from the environment, making it suitable for real-world problems.
- **Exploration of Novel Strategies:**
  - Capable of discovering new strategies that might not be evident with traditional methods.

6. Limitations

- **Sample Efficiency:**
  - RL often requires a large number of interactions with the environment to learn effective policies, which can be computationally expensive.

- **Stability and Convergence:**
    - Training can be unstable and may not always converge to the optimal policy, especially in complex environments.
- **Complexity of Hyperparameter Tuning:**
    - Requires careful tuning of hyperparameters, which can be challenging and time-consuming.
- **Interpretability:**
    - The learned policies can be difficult to interpret, making it hard to understand the decision- making process.

7. Summary

Reinforcement Learning (RL) is a powerful technique for training agents to make decisions through interactions with an environment. By learning from feedback and adjusting actions to maximize rewards, RL can handle complex, dynamic problems and is used in various fields such as game playing, robotics, finance, and healthcare. However, RL requires careful consideration of sample efficiency, stability, and hyperparameter tuning to achieve effective results.

Multi-Armed Bandit

The Multi-Armed Bandit (MAB) problem is a classical problem in probability theory and machine learning, focused on optimizing decision-making in uncertain environments. It's named metaphorically after a slot machine with multiple arms (each arm offering a different payout rate) where the goal is to maximize total rewards over time by choosing the best arm to pull.

1. Concept and Purpose

Multi-Armed Bandit (MAB) Problem:

- **Objective**: To find the optimal strategy for selecting actions (or "arms") from a set of possible options to maximize cumulative rewards over time.
- **Benefit**: Useful in scenarios where you need to balance exploration (trying new options) with exploitation (choosing the best-known option) to optimize outcomes.

2. Key Components

- **Arms**: The different actions or options you can choose from. Each arm has an unknown reward distribution.

- **Rewards**: The payoff received when an arm is pulled. The reward is typically drawn from a probability distribution that is specific to each arm but unknown to the agent.
- **Policy**: The strategy or algorithm used to decide which arm to pull based on the observed rewards and past actions.
- **Exploration vs. Exploitation:**
    - **Exploration**: Trying different arms to gather more information about their reward distributions.
    - **Exploitation**: Choosing the arm with the highest estimated reward based on past experiences.

3. Key Algorithms

1. **ε-Greedy Algorithm:**
    - **Description**: Balances exploration and exploitation by choosing a random arm with probability ε (exploration) and the best-known arm with probability 1-ε (exploitation).
    - **Implementation**:

python

```
import numpy as np

class EpsilonGreedy:
    def __init__(self, n_arms, epsilon):
        self.n_arms = n_arms
        self.epsilon = epsilon
        self.q_values = np.zeros(n_arms)  # Estimated values of arms
        self.action_counts = np.zeros(n_arms)  # Number of times each arm was pulled

    def select_action(self):
        if np.random.rand() < self.epsilon:
            return np.random.randint(self.n_arms)  # Explore
        else:
            return np.argmax(self.q_values)  # Exploit
```

```
    def update(self, action, reward):
        self.action_counts[action] += 1
        self.q_values[action] += (reward - self.q_values[action]) / self.action_counts[action]
```

2. **Upper Confidence Bound (UCB):**

- **Description**: Chooses the arm with the highest upper confidence bound for the estimated reward, balancing exploration and exploitation based on confidence intervals.

Formula:

$$UCB_t(a) = \hat{Q}_t(a) + \sqrt{\frac{2 \ln t}{N_t(a)}}$$

where Q^t(a)\hat{Q}_t(a)Q^t(a) is the estimated reward for arm a, Nt(a)N_t(a)Nt(a) is the number of times arm a has been pulled, and t is the current time step.

- **Implementation**:

python

```python
class UCB:
    def __init__(self, n_arms):
        self.n_arms = n_arms
        self.q_values = np.zeros(n_arms)  # Estimated values of arms
        self.action_counts = np.zeros(n_arms)  # Number of times each arm was pulled
        self.total_counts = 0

    def select_action(self):
        if self.total_counts < self.n_arms:
            return self.total_counts  # Initially pull each arm once
        ucb_values = self.q_values + np.sqrt((2 * np.log(self.total_counts)) / (self.action_counts + 1e-5))
        return np.argmax(ucb_values)

    def update(self, action, reward):
        self.total_counts += 1
        self.action_counts[action] += 1
        self.q_values[action] += (reward - self.q_values[action]) / self.action_counts[action]
```

3. **Thompson Sampling:**
    - **Description**: A Bayesian approach that models the uncertainty of the reward distributions and samples from these distributions to decide which arm to pull.

```
from scipy.stats import beta

class ThompsonSampling:
    def __init__(self, n_arms):
        self.n_arms = n_arms
```

- **Implementation**: Python

```
        self.alpha = np.ones(n_arms)  # Shape parameter for Beta distribution
        self.beta = np.ones(n_arms)   # Rate parameter for Beta distribution

    def select_action(self):
        samples = [beta.rvs(a, b) for a, b in zip(self.alpha, self.beta)]
        return np.argmax(samples)

    def update(self, action, reward):
        if reward == 1:
            self.alpha[action] += 1
        else:
            self.beta[action] += 1
```

4. Applications

- **Online Advertising:**
  - **Objective**: Decide which ads to display to maximize click-through rates and revenue.
- **Recommender Systems:**
  - **Objective**: Select items to recommend to users to maximize user engagement and satisfaction.
- **A/B Testing:**
  - **Objective**: Test different versions of a product or webpage to determine which performs better.
- **Financial Portfolio Management:**
  - **Objective**: Allocate investment resources among different assets to maximize returns.

5. Advantages

- **Simplicity:**
  - MAB algorithms are conceptually simple and easy to implement.
- **Flexibility:**
  - Can be applied to various decision-making problems with uncertain rewards.
- **Balance Between Exploration and Exploitation:**
  - Algorithms like ε-greedy, UCB, and Thompson Sampling effectively manage the exploration- exploitation trade-off.

6. Limitations

- **Limited Context:**
  - MAB problems typically consider each arm independently, ignoring potential context or dependencies between actions.
- **Scalability:**
  - As the number of arms grows, algorithms may become less efficient or require more complex computations.
- **Assumptions:**
  - Some algorithms assume stationary reward distributions, which might not hold in real-world scenarios.

7. Summary

The Multi-Armed Bandit (MAB) problem is a foundational concept in decision theory and machine learning, focusing on optimizing decision-making under uncertainty. Through algorithms such as ε-greedy, Upper Confidence Bound (UCB), and Thompson Sampling, MAB techniques effectively balance exploration and exploitation to maximize cumulative rewards. While MAB offers simplicity and flexibility, it has limitations related to context, scalability, and assumptions about reward distributions. Understanding and applying MAB techniques can enhance decision-making in various practical applications like online advertising, recommender systems, and financial management.

Markov Decision Process (MDP)

A Markov Decision Process (MDP) is a mathematical framework for modeling decision-making in environments with uncertain outcomes. It provides a formalism for understanding and solving problems involving sequential decisions, where each action affects the state of the environment and, consequently, future rewards.

1. Concept and Purpose

Markov Decision Process (MDP):

- **Objective**: To find an optimal policy that maximizes the cumulative reward over time in a given environment.
- **Benefit**: MDPs provide a structured way to address decision-making problems in which outcomes are partly random and partly under the decision-maker's control.

2. Components of an MDP

An MDP is defined by the following components:

1. States (S):
    - A finite set of states S that represent the different possible configurations of the environment.

2. Actions (A):
   - A finite set of actions A available to the agent. The action taken affects the transition from one state to another.
3. **Transition Probability (P):**
   - A probability distribution that specifies the likelihood of transitioning to state s′when action a is taken in state s.

$$P(s'|s,a)$$

4. **Reward Function (R):**
   - A function R(s,a,s′)R(s, a, s')R(s,a,s′) that gives the immediate reward received after transitioning from state s to state s s's′due to action a.
5. **Policy (π):**
   - A policy π(s)π(s)π(s) is a strategy that specifies the action to be taken in each state. It can be deterministic or stochastic.
6. **Value Function (V):**
   - The value function V(s) represents the expected cumulative reward (or return) starting from state s and following a given policy π.
7. **Action-Value Function (Q):**
   - The action-value function Q(s,a)Q(s, a)Q(s,a) represents the expected cumulative reward starting from state s, taking action a, and then following policy π.

3. Key Concepts and Methods

1. **Bellman Equations:**
   - The Bellman equations are recursive formulations that relate the value of a state (or state-action pair) to the values of subsequent states (or state-action pairs).

Bellman Equation for Value Function:

$$V(s) = \sum_{a \in A} \pi(a|s) \sum_{s' \in S} P(s'|s,a) \left[R(s,a,s') + \gamma V(s')\right]$$

Bellman Equation for Action-Value Function:

$$Q(s,a) = \sum_{s' \in S} P(s'|s,a) \left[R(s,a,s') + \gamma \sum_{a' \in A} \pi(a'|s') Q(s',a') \right]$$

where γ is the discount factor representing the importance of future rewards compared to immediate rewards.

2. **Dynamic Programming:**
   - Techniques such as Value Iteration and Policy Iteration use dynamic programming to solve MDPs by iteratively improving estimates of value functions and policies.

- **Value Iteration:**
  - Iteratively updates the value function using the Bellman optimality equation until convergence.
- **Policy Iteration:**
  - Alternates between policy evaluation (calculating the value function for a fixed policy) and policy improvement (updating the policy based on the value function).

3. **Reinforcement Learning Algorithms:**

- In cases where the model of the environment is not known, reinforcement learning algorithms such as Q-learning and SARSA can be used to learn the optimal policy through interactions with the environment.

Q-Learning:

- An off-policy algorithm that learns the optimal action-value function Q∗(s,a)Q^*(s, a)Q∗(s,a) using the Bellman equation for action-values.

SARSA:

- An on-policy algorithm that updates the action-value function based on the action taken and the next action chosen according to the policy.

4. **Policy Gradient Methods:**

- These methods directly optimize the policy by estimating the gradient of the expected reward with respect to the policy parameters. Examples include REINFORCE and Actor-Critic methods.

4. Implementation in Python

Example: Value Iteration using numpy

python

```
import numpy as np

# Define the MDP components
n_states = 3
n_actions = 2
gamma = 0.9
theta = 1e-6

# Initialize state value function
V = np.zeros(n_states)

# Transition probability and reward matrices (example values)
P = np.zeros((n_states, n_actions, n_states))  # Transition probabilities
R = np.zeros((n_states, n_actions, n_states))  # Rewards

# Example transition probabilities and rewards (fill in with actual values)
# ...

def value_iteration():
    global V
    while True:
        delta = 0
        for s in range(n_states):
            v = V[s]
            V[s] = max(sum(P[s, a, s_prime] * (R[s, a, s_prime] + gamma * V[s_prime]) for s_prime in range(n_states)) for a in range(n_actions))
            delta = max(delta, abs(v - V[s]))
        if delta < theta:
            break

value_iteration()
print("Optimal Value Function:", V)
```

Example: Q-Learning using numpy

python

```
import numpy as np

# Define the MDP components
n_states = 5
n_actions = 2
gamma = 0.9
alpha = 0.1  # Learning rate
epsilon = 0.1  # Exploration rate
n_episodes = 1000

# Initialize Q-table
Q = np.zeros((n_states, n_actions))

# Example transition probabilities and rewards (fill in with actual values)
P = np.zeros((n_states, n_actions, n_states))
R = np.zeros((n_states, n_actions, n_states))
```

```
def q_learning():
    for _ in range(n_episodes):
        s = np.random.randint(n_states)
        done = False
        while not done:
            if np.random.rand() < epsilon:
                a = np.random.randint(n_actions)  # Explore
            else:
                a = np.argmax(Q[s])  # Exploit

            next_state = np.random.choice(n_states, p=P[s, a])
            reward = R[s, a, next_state]

            # Q-update
            Q[s, a] += alpha * (reward + gamma * np.max(Q[next_state]) - Q[s, a])


            s = next_state
            done = True  # Or use some condition to terminate episode

q_learning()
print("Optimal Q-Function:", Q)
```

5. Applications

- **Robotics:**
  - MDPs can model tasks such as navigation and manipulation, where the robot must make decisions in uncertain environments.
- **Finance:**
  - Used in portfolio optimization and trading strategies where the goal is to maximize returns over time.
- **Healthcare:**
  - Applied to treatment planning and personalized medicine, decisions must be made over a sequence of stages.
- **Game Playing:**
  - MDPs are used in game AI to make strategic decisions that maximize the chances of winning.
- **Operations Research:**
  - Applied to scheduling, inventory management, and other areas requiring sequential decision-making.

6. Advantages

- **Structured Framework:**
  - Provides a clear and formal way to model decision-making problems with uncertainties.
- **Optimality Guarantees:**
  - Techniques like dynamic programming can provide guarantees of finding the optimal policy under the MDP model.
- Flexibility:
  - Can be adapted to a wide range of problems with different states, actions, and reward structures.

7. Limitations

1. **Computational Complexity:**
   - Solving large MDPs can be computationally expensive due to the need to evaluate a large state- action space.
2. **Assumptions:**
   - Assumes that the MDP model accurately represents the environment, which may not always be the case in real-world scenarios.

3. **Scalability:**
   - Traditional methods like dynamic programming may not scale well for environments with large or continuous state and action spaces.

8. Summary

The Markov Decision Process (MDP) is a powerful tool for modeling and solving decision-making problems where outcomes are uncertain. By formalizing problems in terms of states, actions, rewards, and transitions, MDPs provide a structured approach to finding optimal policies. Techniques such as dynamic programming, reinforcement learning, and policy gradient methods are used to solve MDPs and can be applied to various domains including robotics, finance, healthcare, and game playing. While MDPs offer a robust framework, they come with challenges related to computational complexity, scalability, and the need for accurate modeling of the environment.

Model Predictive Control (MPC)

Model Predictive Control (MPC) is a sophisticated control strategy used in engineering and machine learning for optimizing the control of dynamic systems. MPC leverages a model of the system to predict future states and optimize control actions over a specified horizon. It is widely used in industries such as process control, robotics, automotive, and aerospace due to its ability to handle constraints and optimize performance over time.

1. Concept and Purpose

Model Predictive Control (MPC):

- **Objective**: To compute control actions by solving an optimization problem at each time step, which minimizes a cost function subject to constraints, using a model of the system.
- **Benefit**: MPC optimizes control actions while considering future predictions and constraints, leading to improved system performance and stability.

2. Key Components of MPC

1. **System Model:**
   - A mathematical model of the dynamic system, typically represented by state-space equations or transfer functions.

   - The model is used to predict the future behavior of the system based on current and past states and control inputs.

2. **Prediction Horizon (N):**
   - The time frame over which future states are predicted. The length of the horizon influences the trade-off between computational complexity and control performance.
3. **Control Horizon (Nc):**
   - The time frame over which control actions are optimized. It is usually shorter than the prediction horizon.
4. **Cost Function (J):**
   - A function that quantifies the performance of the control strategy, typically involving terms for tracking error and control effort. Commonly used cost functions include quadratic forms of state deviations and control inputs: where xrefx_{ref}xref is the reference trajectory, Q and R are weighting matrices for state and control inputs respectively.

$$J = \sum_{k=0}^{N-1} \left(\|x_{k+1} - x_{ref}\|_Q^2 + \|u_k\|_R^2 \right)$$

5. **Constraints:**
   - **State Constraints:** Bounds on the state variables.
   - **Input Constraints:** Limits on the control inputs.
   - **Terminal Constraints:** Constraints on the state or control input at the end of the prediction horizon to ensure stability.

3. How MPC Works

- **Formulate the Optimization Problem:**
   - At each control step, MPC solves an optimization problem to find the sequence of control inputs that minimizes the cost function while satisfying constraints.
   - This typically involves solving a constrained quadratic programming (QP) problem.
- **Apply the First Control Action:**
   - Implement the first control input of the optimized sequence.

- **Recompute at Each Step:**
  - At the next time step, update the system state with new measurements, and re-solve the optimization problem using the updated state.
- **Feedback Mechanism:**
  - The process is repeated, providing a feedback loop that continually adjusts the control inputs based on the latest state information.

4. Implementation in Python

Example: MPC for a Simple Linear System

python

```
import numpy as np
import cvxpy as cp


# System parameters
A = np.array([[1.1, 0.2], [0.1, 0.9]])  # System matrix
B = np.array([[0.1], [0.2]])  # Input matrix
```

```
C = np.array([[1, 0]])  # Output matrix
Q = np.eye(2)  # State weight matrix
R = np.eye(1)  # Control weight matrix
N = 10  # Prediction horizon
Nc = 2  # Control horizon

# MPC parameters
x0 = np.array([[0], [0]])  # Initial state
xref = np.array([[1], [1]])  # Reference state

# Variables
x = cp.Variable((2, N+1))  # State trajectory
u = cp.Variable((1, N))    # Control trajectory

# Cost function
cost = 0
constraints = []

for k in range(N):
    cost += cp.quad_form(x[:, k] - xref.flatten(), Q) + cp.quad_form(u[:, k], R)
    constraints += [x[:, k+1] == A @ x[:, k] + B @ u[:, k]]  # State dynamics
    constraints += [cp.norm(u[:, k], 'inf') <= 1]  # Input constraint

# Terminal constraints
constraints += [x[:, N] == A @ x[:, N-1] + B @ u[:, N-1]]  # Terminal state

# Optimization problem
prob = cp.Problem(cp.Minimize(cost), constraints)

# Solve the optimization problem
prob.solve()

# Extract the optimal control input
optimal_u = u[:, 0].value
print("Optimal Control Input:", optimal_u)
```

5. Applications

- **Process Control:**
  - MPC is used in chemical, petrochemical, and manufacturing industries to regulate processes such as temperature, pressure, and concentration.
- **Robotics:**
  - Used for trajectory planning and control in robotic systems, including robotic arms and autonomous vehicles.
- **Automotive:**
  - Applied in advanced driver assistance systems (ADAS) and autonomous driving for trajectory optimization and control.
- **Aerospace:**
  - Utilized for flight control systems to manage the dynamics of aircraft and spacecraft.
- **Energy Systems:**
  - MPC is used to control power grids, optimize energy usage in smart grids, and manage renewable energy sources.

5. Advantages

- **Handling Constraints:**
  - MPC can explicitly handle constraints on states and control inputs, making it suitable for complex systems.
- **Optimizing Performance:**
  - MPC improves overall system performance and stability by predicting future states and optimizing control actions.
- **Flexibility:**
  - Applicable to a wide range of systems, from linear to nonlinear, and can be adapted to various operational conditions.

6. Limitations

- **Computational Complexity:**
  - Solving the optimization problem at each time step can be computationally intensive, particularly for large systems.
- **Model Dependence:**
  - The performance of MPC depends on the accuracy of the system model. Inaccurate models can degrade performance.

- **Real-Time Constraints:**
  - Ensuring that the optimization problem is solved quickly enough can be challenging in real-time applications.

7. Summary

Model Predictive Control (MPC) is a powerful and versatile control technique used for optimizing dynamic systems under constraints. By using a model to predict future behavior and solve an optimization problem at each time step, MPC provides a robust framework for managing complex control problems. While MPC offers significant advantages in handling constraints and optimizing performance, it also presents challenges related to computational complexity and model accuracy. Understanding and implementing MPC effectively can enhance the control of various systems, including industrial processes, robotics, and autonomous vehicles.

Randomized control

Randomized control techniques in machine learning typically involve methods where randomness plays a key role in improving performance, exploration, and robustness. These techniques are often used in scenarios where decision-making involves uncertainty, such as in reinforcement learning, algorithm design, and control systems.

1. Concept and Purpose

Randomized Control Techniques:

- **Objective**: To enhance decision-making processes and control strategies by incorporating randomness, leading to improved exploration, robustness, and performance in various applications.
- **Benefit**: Randomized approaches can provide better solutions in complex environments, help avoid local optima, and enable efficient exploration of large state spaces.

2. Key Techniques Involving Randomized Control

1. **Randomized Algorithms:**
    - **Definition**: Algorithms that use randomness to improve performance or simplify problem- solving. They can offer

expected performance guarantees or improved solution quality compared to deterministic algorithms.
   - **Example**: Randomized QuickSort, where randomness in selecting the pivot improves average- case performance.
2. **Randomized Optimization:**
   - **Definition**: Optimization methods that incorporate randomness to explore the solution space more effectively and avoid getting stuck in local optima.
   - **Example**: Simulated Annealing, which uses randomness to escape local minima by probabilistically accepting worse solutions with decreasing likelihood over time.
3. **Stochastic Control:**
   - **Definition**: Control methods incorporating random variables or stochastic processes into the control strategy to handle uncertainty and improve performance in dynamic environments.
   - **Example**: Stochastic Model Predictive Control (SMPC), which extends traditional MPC by considering uncertainty in the model predictions.
4. **Exploration Strategies in Reinforcement Learning:**
   - **Definition**: Techniques in reinforcement learning that use randomness to balance exploration (trying new actions) and exploitation (choosing known optimal actions).
   - **Example**: ε-greedy strategy, where actions are chosen randomly with probability ε, while the best-known action is chosen with probability 1 - ε.
5. **Randomized Policy Search:**
   - **Definition**: Methods for learning control policies by exploring random policies and evaluating their performance to find an effective policy.
   - **Example**: Random Search, where a policy is randomly generated and tested, and the best- performing policies are used to guide further exploration.

3. Detailed Examples

1. **Simulated Annealing:**

Simulated Annealing is a randomized optimization technique inspired by the annealing process in metallurgy. It uses randomness to escape local optima and gradually converges to a global optimum.

Algorithm Steps:

1. **Initialization**: Start with an initial solution and temperature.
2. **Generate Neighbor**: Randomly perturb the current solution to generate a neighbor.
3. **Evaluate**: Compute the cost of the neighbor solution.
4. **Acceptance Criteria**: If the neighbor solution is better, accept it. If it's worse, accept it with a probability that decreases with temperature.
5. **Update**: Reduce the temperature according to a cooling schedule.
6. **Repeat**: Continue until convergence criteria are met.

Python Implementation Example:

Python

```
import numpy as np

def objective_function(x):
    return x**2

def simulated_annealing(initial_solution, temperature, cooling_rate, num_iterations):
    current_solution = initial_solution
    best_solution = current_solution
    best_cost = objective_function(best_solution)

    for i in range(num_iterations):
        new_solution = current_solution + np.random.uniform(-1, 1)
        current_cost = objective_function(current_solution)
        new_cost = objective_function(new_solution)

        if new_cost < current_cost or np.random.rand() < np.exp((current_cost - new_cost) / temperature):
            current_solution = new_solution
            if new_cost < best_cost:
                best_solution = new_solution
                best_cost = new_cost

        temperature *= cooling_rate

    return best_solution, best_cost

# Parameters
initial_solution = 10
temperature = 1.0
cooling_rate = 0.99
num_iterations = 1000

best_solution, best_cost = simulated_annealing(initial_solution, temperature, cooling_rate, num_iterations)
print(f"Best Solution: {best_solution}, Best Cost: {best_cost}")
```

2. ε-Greedy Strategy in Reinforcement Learning:

The ε-greedy strategy is used to balance exploration and exploitation in reinforcement learning. It selects a

random action with probability ε and the best-known action with probability 1 - ε.

Python Implementation Example:

Python

```
import numpy as np

def objective_function(x):
    return x**2

def simulated_annealing(initial_solution, temperature, cooling_rate, num_iterations):
    current_solution = initial_solution
    best_solution = current_solution
    best_cost = objective_function(best_solution)

    for i in range(num_iterations):
        new_solution = current_solution + np.random.uniform(-1, 1)
        current_cost = objective_function(current_solution)
        new_cost = objective_function(new_solution)

        if new_cost < current_cost or np.random.rand() < np.exp((current_cost - new_cost) / temperature):
            current_solution = new_solution
            if new_cost < best_cost:
                best_solution = new_solution
                best_cost = new_cost

        temperature *= cooling_rate

    return best_solution, best_cost

# Parameters
initial_solution = 10
temperature = 1.0
cooling_rate = 0.99
num_iterations = 1000

best_solution, best_cost = simulated_annealing(initial_solution, temperature, cooling_rate, num_iterations)
print(f"Best Solution: {best_solution}, Best Cost: {best_cost}")
```

4. Applications

- **Robotics:**
  - Randomized control can help in path planning and exploration tasks where exact models are challenging to define.
- **Automotive:**
  - Used in autonomous vehicles for exploration and improving decision-making under uncertainty.
- **Optimization Problems:**
  - Applied to complex optimization problems where traditional methods may fail to find optimal solutions efficiently.

- **Game Playing:**
  - Randomized strategies are used in game AI to create diverse and unpredictable behaviors.
- **Financial Systems:**
  - Randomized algorithms and stochastic control are used for risk management and optimizing trading strategies.

5. Advantages

- **Improved Exploration:**
  - Randomized methods can explore a broader range of possibilities and avoid getting stuck in local optima.
- Flexibility:
  - Applicable to a wide range of problems with different levels of complexity and uncertainty.
- **Simplicity:**
  - Often simpler to implement and understand compared to deterministic methods.

6. Limitations

- **Performance Guarantees:**
  - The performance of randomized methods can be less predictable and may not guarantee optimal solutions.
- **Parameter Tuning:**
  - Randomized methods often require careful tuning of parameters such as ε in ε-greedy or temperature in simulated annealing.
- **Computational Cost:**
  - Randomized methods may require a large number of iterations or samples to achieve good performance, leading to higher computational costs.

7. Summary

Randomized control techniques leverage randomness to improve decision-making, exploration, and optimization. By incorporating randomness into algorithms and control strategies, these methods can offer significant advantages in terms of flexibility, exploration, and robustness. They are widely used in various fields, including reinforcement learning, robotics, optimization, and game playing. However, they also come with challenges, such as the need for parameter tuning and the lack of guaranteed performance. Understanding and applying randomized control techniques effectively can lead to better solutions in complex and uncertain environments.

Synthetic Control

Synthetic Control is a method used in machine learning and econometrics to evaluate the effect of an intervention or treatment by comparing an affected unit to a synthetic control group created from a weighted combination of untreated units. This technique is especially useful in observational studies where randomized control trials are not feasible. It allows for robust causal inference by creating a counterfactual scenario to estimate what would have happened to the treated unit if the intervention had not occurred.

1. Concept and Purpose

Synthetic Control Method:

- **Objective**: To estimate the causal effect of an intervention by constructing a synthetic version of the treated unit from a weighted average of control units that did not receive the intervention.
- **Benefit**: Provides a rigorous and data-driven approach to estimating treatment effects, particularly when traditional methods struggle with confounding factors or lack of appropriate control groups.

2. Key Components of Synthetic Control

1. **Treatment Unit:**
    - The unit (e.g., a country, city, company) that receives the intervention or treatment.
2. **Control Units:**
    - Units that do not receive the intervention and are used to construct the synthetic control group.
3. **Outcome Variable:**
    - The variable of interest that is affected by the treatment. It is measured for both the treated and control units.
4. **Pre-Treatment Data:**
    - Data on the outcome variable and potentially other covariates before the intervention. This data is used to match the treated unit with the synthetic control.
5. **Synthetic Control:**
    - A weighted combination of control units constructed to approximate the pre-treatment characteristics of the treated unit. The weights are chosen to minimize the difference between the pre-treatment characteristics of the treated unit and the synthetic control.

3. How Synthetic Control Works

1. **Select Control Units:**
    - Identify a set of units that did not receive the intervention and could potentially be used to construct the synthetic control.
2. **Define Pre-Treatment Characteristics:**
    - Collect data on the outcome variable and other relevant covariates for both the treated and control units prior to the intervention.
3. **Construct Synthetic Control:**
    - Use a weighted average of the control units to create a synthetic version of the treated unit. The weights are chosen to minimize the distance between the pre-treatment characteristics of the treated unit and the synthetic control.
4. **Estimate Treatment Effect:**
    - Compare the post-treatment outcomes of the treated unit to the outcomes of the synthetic control. The difference is used to estimate the causal effect of the intervention.

4. Example in Python

Example: Evaluating the Impact of a Policy Intervention

Python

```python
import numpy as np
import pandas as pd
from sklearn.linear_model import LinearRegression
from scipy.optimize import minimize

# Example data
# Columns: 'unit', 'time', 'outcome', 'covariate1', 'covariate2'
data = pd.DataFrame({
    'unit': ['A'] * 10 + ['B'] * 10 + ['C'] * 10,
    'time': list(range(10)) * 3,
    'outcome': np.random.rand(30),
    'covariate1': np.random.rand(30),
    'covariate2': np.random.rand(30),
})

# Pre-treatment period (e.g., first 5 time periods)
pre_treatment_data = data[data['time'] < 5]

# Post-treatment period (e.g., last 5 time periods)
post_treatment_data = data[data['time'] >= 5]

# Define the treatment unit and control units
treatment_unit = 'A'
control_units = ['B', 'C']

# Pre-treatment characteristics
X_pre_treatment = pre_treatment_data[pre_treatment_data['unit'] == treatment_unit][['covariate1', 'covariate2']].values
X_controls = pre_treatment_data[pre_treatment_data['unit'].isin(control_units)][['covariate1', 'covariate2']].values

# Construct the synthetic control
def objective_function(weights):
    synthetic_control = np.dot(weights, X_controls)
    return np.sum((X_pre_treatment - synthetic_control) ** 2)

initial_weights = np.ones(len(control_units)) / len(control_units)
constraints = {'type': 'eq', 'fun': lambda w: np.sum(w) - 1}
bounds = [(0, 1)] * len(control_units)
result = minimize(objective_function, initial_weights, bounds=bounds, constraints=constraints)
synthetic_weights = result.x

# Post-treatment outcomes
outcomes_treatment = post_treatment_data[post_treatment_data['unit'] == treatment_unit]['outcome'].values
outcomes_synthetic_control = np.dot(synthetic_weights, post_treatment_data[post_treatment_data['unit'].isin(control_units)]['outcome'].values)

# Estimate the treatment effect
treatment_effect = np.mean(outcomes_treatment) - np.mean(outcomes_synthetic_control)
print(f"Estimated Treatment Effect: {treatment_effect}")
```

5. Applications

1. **Economics and Public Policy:**
   - Used to evaluate the impact of policy changes, economic reforms, or other interventions on various outcomes such as GDP, employment, and crime rates.

2. **Healthcare:**
    - Applied to assess the effects of new treatments or health interventions by comparing treated populations to synthetic controls.
3. **Environmental Studies:**
    - Helps to understand the impact of environmental policies or events on environmental indicators.
4. Business and Marketing:
    - Used to measure the effectiveness of marketing campaigns or business interventions by comparing treated units (e.g., stores, regions) to synthetic controls.

6. Advantages

1. **Robust Causal Inference:**
    - Provides a rigorous method for causal inference by creating a counterfactual scenario based on observable data.
2. **Flexibility:**
    - Can be applied to a wide range of applications and interventions.
3. **No Randomization Required:**
    - Useful in observational studies where random assignment is not possible.

7. Limitations

1. **Data Requirements:**
    - Requires a sufficient number of control units and pre-treatment data to create a reliable synthetic control.
2. Model Dependence:
    - The quality of the synthetic control depends on the model used to estimate it and the choice of control units.
3. Assumptions:
    - Assumes that the synthetic control is a valid counterfactual and that the pre-treatment characteristics of the treated unit can be well approximated by the synthetic control.

8. Summary

Synthetic Control is a powerful technique for evaluating the impact of interventions by constructing a counterfactual scenario from a weighted combination of control units. It provides a robust framework for causal inference in observational studies and is applicable in various fields, including economics, healthcare, and business. While it offers significant advantages in terms of causal analysis and flexibility, it also has limitations related to data requirements and model dependence. Understanding and applying Synthetic Control effectively can lead to more accurate assessments of the effects of interventions and policies.

Case Study and Adoption Across Domains World Wide

No	Domains	ML Adoption Topics
1	Ecommerce	Ecommerce Market Place
2	Ecommerce	Transforming eCommerce Product Segmentation with Machine Learning
3	Ecommerce	Improving E-Commerce Sales Using Machine Learning
4	Energy	Energy research
5	Energy	Forecasting Face-off for Oil and Gas Spare Parts
6	Finance	Financial Risk Management
7	Finance	Stock market research
8	Finance	GAN-Based Market Simulation for Derivatives Pricing and Dynamic Hedging
9	Finance	Consumer Credit Risk
10	Finance	Consumer Credit Analysis
11	Finance	Occupations and the Economy
12	Finance	Comparison and Financial Assessment of Demand Forecasting Methodologies for seasonal CPGs
13	Insurance	Insurance Claims
14	IT systems	Systems Theory Approach to Cyber securing a Supervised Machine Learning System
15	IT Systems	Poisoning Cyberattacks
16	Market	Real Estate
17	Market	Sales and customer segments
18	Market	Invoice-to-Cash Collection Through Machine Learning
19	Medical	Neural networks to understand intricate patterns of human interaction
20	Medical	Medical Science
21	Medical	Conventional clinical methods in guiding management of heart failure patients Machine Learning
22	Medical	Neuroimaging to Improve Brain Health Machine Learning
23	Medical	Inferring Primary Care Relationships
24	Medical	Prediction of Cardiovascular Death After Acute Coronary Syndrome
25	Medical	Continuously monitored physiological data
26	Medical	Patient Selection for Cardiac Resynchronization Therapy
27	Medical	Gesture Recognition Toolkit
28	Medical	Biological Networks using Machine Learning
29	Medical	Drug discovery
30	Medical	Trace Genetically Engineered DNA
31	Retail	Retail order management
32	Retail	Demand Planning
33	Retail	Forecasting Seasonal Footwear Demand
34	Retail	Predicting Shipping Time
35	Retail	Approaches to Improve Long-Range Demand Forecasting
36	Retail	Radio Frequency Integrated Circuits (RFIC) Development using machine learning
37	Scientific	Materials science using supervised machine learning
38	Scientific	Predicting Material Properties Interatomic Potentials
39	Scientific	Predictive Maintenance of Wind Turbines
40	Scientific	Oceanic eddy detection and lifetime forecast using machine learning
41	Social	Demographic Bias Detection and Analysis
42	Social	Social Inductive Biases for Reinforcement Learning
43	Social	Program Synthesis for Social Recommendations
44	Social	Socially Guided Machine Learning
45	Social	Election Exit Poll

E-commerce Market Place Machine Learning

Machine learning (ML) is transforming eCommerce marketplaces by enhancing customer experiences, optimizing operations, and driving sales. Here's an overview of key applications, techniques, and considerations for implementing ML in this domain.

Key Applications

1. **Personalization**:
   - **Product Recommendations**: Use collaborative filtering and content-based filtering to recommend products to users based on their browsing and purchasing history.
   - **Dynamic Pricing**: Implement algorithms that adjust prices based on demand, competition, and customer behavior to maximize sales.
2. **Customer Segmentation**:
   - Analyze customer data to segment users based on purchasing behavior, preferences, and demographics, enabling targeted marketing campaigns.
3. **Search Optimization**:
   - Improve search algorithms using natural language processing (NLP) to understand user queries better and deliver more relevant search results.

1. **Fraud Detection**:
   - Use anomaly detection techniques to identify fraudulent transactions and behaviors, protecting both the marketplace and its users.
2. **Churn Prediction**:
   - Analyze customer interactions to predict which users are likely to stop using the platform, enabling proactive engagement strategies to retain them.
3. **Inventory Management**:
   - Forecast demand for products using historical sales data, optimizing inventory levels and reducing overstock or stockouts.
4. **Sentiment Analysis**:
   - Analyze customer reviews and feedback to gauge sentiment and identify areas for improvement in products and services.
5. **Customer Service Automation**:
   - Implement chatbots powered by NLP to handle customer inquiries and support requests, improving response times and satisfaction.

Techniques

1. **Supervised Learning**:
   - **Classification Models**: Use algorithms like decision trees, random forests, and logistic regression to classify customer segments or predict churn.
   - **Regression Models**: Apply regression techniques to predict sales and demand based on historical data.
2. **Unsupervised Learning**:
   - **Clustering**: Use K-means or hierarchical clustering to segment customers based on behavior and preferences.
   - **Dimensionality Reduction**: Implement techniques like PCA to simplify data and highlight key features.
3. **Deep Learning**:
   - **Neural Networks**: Use deep learning models for complex tasks like image recognition (e.g., for product images) and NLP for understanding customer queries.
   - **Recurrent Neural Networks (RNNs)**: Apply RNNs for sequence prediction tasks, such as forecasting future purchases based on historical data.

4. **Natural Language Processing (NLP)**:
    - Utilize NLP for search optimization, sentiment analysis, and chatbots to improve user interactions.
5. **Reinforcement Learning**:
    - Apply RL to optimize recommendation systems and dynamic pricing strategies based on user interactions.

Considerations

1. **Data Privacy and Security**:
    - Ensure compliance with regulations such as GDPR to protect user data and maintain customer trust.
2. **Bias and Fairness**:
    - Address potential biases in ML algorithms to ensure fair treatment of all users and avoid discrimination in recommendations or pricing.
3. **Scalability**:
    - Design ML models and infrastructure that can scale as the marketplace grows and data volume increases.
4. **Integration with Existing Systems**:
    - Ensure that ML solutions integrate seamlessly with existing eCommerce platforms and workflows to enhance usability.
5. **Model Interpretability**:
    - Use interpretable models or techniques to explain recommendations and predictions to stakeholders, fostering trust in the system.
6. **Continuous Improvement**:
    - Implement feedback loops to continuously monitor and improve ML models based on user interactions and changing market conditions.

Conclusion

Machine learning is a powerful tool for enhancing eCommerce marketplaces by personalizing user experiences, optimizing operations, and driving revenue growth. By leveraging various ML techniques and maintaining a focus on ethical considerations, eCommerce businesses can gain a competitive edge and improve customer satisfaction. Ongoing research and collaboration across disciplines will be crucial to unlocking the full potential of ML in this dynamic field.

Transforming eCommerce Product Segmentation

In the fast-paced world of eCommerce, effectively segmenting products is key to understanding market dynamics and meeting customer needs. Machine learning (ML) algorithms can significantly enhance product segmentation by providing insights that drive personalized marketing strategies, inventory management, and customer engagement. Here's a comprehensive guide to implementing ML algorithms for eCommerce product segmentation.

Key Steps in Implementing ML for Product Segmentation

1. **Data Collection**
   - Gather data from various sources:
     - **Product Data:** Features like category, price, specifications, images, and descriptions.
     - **Customer Data:** Purchase history, browsing behavior, demographic information, and customer reviews.
2. **Data Preprocessing**
   - Clean the data:
     - Handle missing values and remove duplicates.
     - Normalize and standardize features to ensure consistency.
   - Convert categorical variables into numerical formats using techniques like one-hot encoding.

1. **Feature Engineering**
    - Extract relevant features that may influence product performance:
        - **Product Features:** Price ranges, product ratings, and sales volume.
        - **Customer Features:** Frequency of purchases, average basket size, and interaction with product categories.
2. **Selecting Machine Learning Algorithms**
    - Choose appropriate algorithms based on the type of segmentation needed. Here are some commonly used techniques:
    - **Clustering Algorithms:**
        - **K-Means Clustering:**
            - A widely used algorithm that partitions products into K distinct clusters based on feature similarity.
            - Steps:
                1. Select the number of clusters (K).
                2. Initialize cluster centroids randomly.
                3. Assign products to the nearest centroid.
                4. Update centroids based on the mean of assigned products.
                5. Repeat until convergence.
        - **Hierarchical Clustering:**
            - Builds a tree of clusters (dendrogram), allowing for different levels of granularity.
            - Useful for visualizing product relationships.
        - **DBSCAN (Density-Based Spatial Clustering of Applications with Noise):**
            - Identifies clusters based on the density of points, useful for discovering non-linear patterns and noise.
    - **Dimensionality Reduction:**
        - **Principal Component Analysis (PCA):**
            - Reduces the dimensionality of the dataset while preserving variance, making clustering more effective.
    - **Deep Learning Approaches:**
        - **Autoencoders:**
            - Neural networks that learn to compress and reconstruct data, useful for feature extraction before clustering.

- **Convolutional Neural Networks (CNNs):**
  - Particularly effective for image data, enabling segmentation based on visual attributes.

1. **Model Training and Validation**
   - Split the dataset into training and test sets.
   - Train the selected algorithms on the training set.
   - Validate model performance using metrics such as:
     - **Silhouette Score:** Measures how similar an object is to its own cluster compared to other clusters.
     - **Davies-Bouldin Index:** Evaluates the average similarity ratio of each cluster with the one that is most similar.
2. **Applying the Model**
   - Once trained, apply the model to the entire product dataset to generate segments.
   - Analyze the characteristics of each segment to inform marketing and inventory strategies.
3. **Integration and Continuous Improvement**
   - Integrate segmentation results into marketing campaigns, product recommendations, and inventory management systems.
   - Continuously monitor performance and gather feedback to refine the segmentation process over time.

Applications of Machine Learning in Product Segmentation

1. **Personalized Marketing:**
   - Tailor promotions and advertisements to specific product segments, enhancing customer engagement.
2. **Dynamic Pricing Strategies:**
   - Use segmented data to inform pricing strategies based on demand elasticity and customer profiles.
3. **Inventory Optimization:**
   - Adjust stock levels based on predicted demand for segmented product categories.
4. **Enhanced Customer Experience:**
   - Create dynamic websites that showcase products relevant to individual customer segments.
5. **Trend Analysis:**
   - Identify emerging trends by analyzing customer preferences within each product segment.

Challenges and Considerations

- **Data Quality:** Ensure the data is accurate, complete, and representative of the customer base.
- **Interpretability:** Use interpretable models or techniques like SHAP to explain clustering results to stakeholders.
- **Scalability:** Ensure ML solutions can handle increasing product and customer data volumes.
- **Ethical Considerations:** Address potential biases in data that may affect segmentation outcomes.

Conclusion

Transforming eCommerce product segmentation using machine learning algorithms allows businesses to gain deeper insights into their offerings and customer preferences. By leveraging these advanced techniques, companies can enhance their marketing strategies, improve inventory management, and deliver personalized shopping experiences. As eCommerce continues to evolve, the strategic application of ML in product segmentation will be essential for maintaining a competitive edge in the market.

Improving E-Commerce Sales Using Machine Learning

Machine learning (ML) has become a transformative tool in e-commerce, enabling businesses to enhance sales through personalized experiences, efficient inventory management, and targeted marketing strategies. Here's an overview of how ML can improve e-commerce sales:

Key Applications

1. **Personalized Recommendations**
   - **Collaborative Filtering**: Analyzing user behavior to recommend products based on similar customers' preferences.
   - **Content-Based Filtering**: Suggesting products based on attributes and features of items previously purchased or viewed by the customer.
2. **Dynamic Pricing**
   - **Price Optimization**: Using ML algorithms to analyze market demand, competitor pricing, and customer behavior to adjust prices in real-time for maximum sales and profitability.
   - **Demand Forecasting**: Predicting product demand to optimize pricing strategies and inventory levels.
3. **Customer Segmentation**
   - **Behavioral Clustering**: Segmenting customers based on purchasing behavior, demographics, and engagement levels to tailor marketing efforts and promotions.

- **Churn Prediction**: Identifying customers at risk of leaving and implementing targeted retention strategies.

4. **Fraud Detection**
   - **Anomaly Detection**: Employing ML algorithms to detect unusual transaction patterns that may indicate fraudulent activity, helping to reduce losses and build trust.
5. **Chatbots and Virtual Assistants**
   - **Customer Support**: Using natural language processing (NLP) and ML to power chatbots that provide instant responses to customer inquiries, enhancing user experience and satisfaction.
6. **Inventory Management**
   - **Stock Level Optimization**: Using predictive analytics to forecast inventory needs, minimizing stockouts and excess inventory.
   - **Supply Chain Optimization**: Analyzing data from suppliers, market trends, and sales history to improve supply chain efficiency.
7. **Sentiment Analysis**
   - **Review and Feedback Analysis**: Analyzing customer reviews and social media sentiment to gain insights into customer satisfaction and product performance, informing marketing strategies.

Techniques Used

1. **Supervised Learning**
   - Algorithms such as decision trees, random forests, and gradient boosting are used for predictive tasks like customer segmentation and sales forecasting.
2. **Unsupervised Learning**
   - Clustering techniques (e.g., K-means, DBSCAN) help in identifying distinct customer segments based on purchasing behavior.
3. **Deep Learning**
   - Neural networks, especially recurrent neural networks (RNNs) and convolutional neural networks (CNNs), effectively handle complex data patterns, such as image recognition for product recommendations.

1. **Natural Language Processing (NLP)**
    - NLP is applied in sentiment analysis, chatbots, and understanding customer queries to improve service and product recommendations.

Benefits

- **Increased Sales**: Personalized recommendations and targeted marketing can significantly boost conversion rates and average order value.
- **Enhanced Customer Experience**: Tailored experiences lead to higher customer satisfaction and loyalty, fostering repeat business.
- **Operational Efficiency**: Improved inventory management and fraud detection enhance operational workflows, reducing costs and risks.
- **Data-Driven Decisions**: Insights derived from ML analyses allow for more informed strategic decisions.

Challenges and Considerations

1. **Data Quality and Integration**
    - High-quality, relevant data is essential for effective ML applications. Integrating data from various sources can be challenging.
2. **Interpretability**
    - Some ML models, particularly complex ones, may act as "black boxes," making it difficult for stakeholders to understand and trust their predictions.
3. **Privacy and Security**
    - Handling customer data responsibly is crucial, especially in light of regulations like GDPR. Businesses must ensure data security and user consent.
4. **Implementation Costs**
    - Developing and deploying ML solutions can require significant investment in technology and expertise.

Conclusion

Machine learning offers powerful tools for improving e-commerce sales through personalization, optimization, and enhanced customer interactions. By leveraging these technologies, e-commerce businesses can create more engaging shopping experiences, optimize operations, and drive revenue growth. Continuous adaptation to market trends and customer preferences, combined with ethical data practices, will be vital for sustained success in the evolving e-commerce landscape.

Energy research Machine Learning

Machine learning (ML) is transforming energy research by optimizing energy consumption, improving renewable energy integration, and enhancing predictive maintenance. Here's an overview of key applications, techniques, and considerations for using ML in this domain.

Key Applications

1. **Demand Forecasting**:
    - **Load Prediction**: Use historical consumption data to predict future energy demand, allowing for better grid management and resource allocation.
    - **Seasonality and Trends**: Incorporate seasonal variations and economic indicators into demand forecasting models.
2. **Renewable Energy Integration**:
    - **Production Forecasting**: Predict energy generation from renewable sources (solar, wind) using weather data and historical generation patterns.
    - **Grid Management**: Optimize the integration of renewable energy into the grid by predicting fluctuations in supply and demand.
3. **Energy Efficiency Optimization**:
    - **Building Energy Management**: Use ML to analyze

building energy usage patterns and recommend improvements for energy efficiency.
    - **Smart Grids**: Implement ML algorithms to optimize energy distribution and usage in smart grids.
4. **Predictive Maintenance**:
    - **Equipment Failure Prediction**: Analyze sensor data from equipment (e.g., turbines, generators) to predict and prevent failures, reducing downtime and maintenance costs.
    - **Condition Monitoring**: Use ML for real-time monitoring of equipment conditions to anticipate maintenance needs.
5. **Energy Trading and Market Analysis**:
    - **Price Prediction**: Utilize ML algorithms to forecast energy prices based on market conditions, demand, and supply factors.
    - **Trading Strategies**: Develop algorithmic trading strategies for energy markets using historical data and predictive models.
6. **Anomaly Detection**:
    - Identify unusual patterns in energy consumption that may indicate inefficiencies or potential issues, such as leaks or equipment failures.

Techniques

1. **Supervised Learning**:
    - **Regression Models**: Predict energy demand and generation using regression techniques like linear regression, decision trees, or support vector regression.
    - **Classification Algorithms**: Classify different energy usage patterns or predict equipment failures.
2. **Unsupervised Learning**:
    - **Clustering**: Group similar energy consumption patterns to identify trends and optimize resource allocation.
    - **Dimensionality Reduction**: Use techniques like PCA to analyze large datasets and identify key features affecting energy usage.
3. **Time Series Analysis**:
    - **ARIMA Models**: Traditional time series forecasting methods for demand and generation prediction.
    - **LSTM Networks**: Use long short-term memory networks for

more complex time series data, capturing temporal dependencies.

4. **Reinforcement Learning**:
   - Apply RL techniques to optimize energy consumption in smart grids and develop adaptive control strategies.
5. **Deep Learning**:
   - Use neural networks for complex pattern recognition in energy consumption data or weather forecasting.

Considerations

1. **Data Quality**:
   - Ensure high-quality, reliable data for training models. Data preprocessing and cleaning are crucial steps.
2. **Feature Engineering**:
   - Identify and create relevant features that capture the dynamics of energy consumption, weather effects, and economic factors.
3. **Model Interpretability**:
   - Use interpretable models or explainability techniques (like SHAP or LIME) to communicate model predictions and insights effectively.
4. **Integration with Existing Systems**:
   - Ensure ML solutions can be seamlessly integrated with existing energy management systems and infrastructure.
5. **Scalability**:
   - Choose models and infrastructure that can scale as data volume and complexity increase.
6. **Regulatory Compliance**:
   - Adhere to regulations regarding data usage and energy market operations.

Conclusion

Machine learning holds significant promise for advancing energy research, enhancing efficiency, and facilitating the transition to sustainable energy systems. By leveraging data effectively and implementing robust ML techniques, researchers and energy providers can optimize operations, improve decision-making, and support the integration of renewable energy sources. Continuous research and collaboration will be essential to unlock the full potential of ML in this rapidly evolving field.

Forecasting Face-off for Oil and Gas Spare Parts

In the oil and gas industry, managing spare parts inventory effectively is crucial for minimizing downtime and ensuring operational efficiency. Machine learning (ML) can enhance forecasting accuracy for spare parts demand, allowing companies to optimize inventory levels and reduce costs. Here's an overview of how ML can be applied in this context.

Key Objectives

1. **Demand Forecasting:** Predict future demand for spare parts based on historical data and external factors.
2. **Inventory Optimization:** Ensures that the right amount of spare parts is available at the right time, reducing excess inventory and stockouts.
3. **Maintenance Planning:** Align spare parts availability with maintenance schedules and operational needs.

Data Sources

- **Historical Demand Data:** Past usage patterns of spare parts, including frequency and quantity.
- **Operational Data:** Information on equipment performance, maintenance schedules, and operational conditions.

- **Supply Chain Data:** Lead times for spare parts, supplier reliability, and logistics information.
- **External Factors:** Economic indicators, oil prices, and weather conditions that may affect demand.

Applications of Machine Learning

1. **Time Series Forecasting:**
    - **ARIMA (AutoRegressive Integrated Moving Average):** A traditional statistical approach for forecasting demand based on historical data.
    - **LSTM (Long Short-Term Memory) Networks:** A type of recurrent neural network suitable for capturing temporal dependencies in time series data.
2. **Predictive Analytics:**
    - **Regression Models:** Used to predict the demand for spare parts based on multiple features, such as equipment usage and external conditions.
    - **Ensemble Learning:** Techniques like Random Forests or Gradient Boosting Machines can improve forecasting accuracy by combining multiple models.
3. **Clustering and Segmentation:**
    - **K-means Clustering:** Group spare parts into categories based on usage patterns, which helps tailor forecasting models to different segments.
    - **Hierarchical Clustering:** Identify relationships between different spare parts and their demand profiles.
4. **Anomaly Detection:**
    - Identify outliers in demand data that may indicate unusual events, such as equipment failures or sudden increases in operational activity.

Techniques Used

1. **Supervised Learning:**
    - **Classification and Regression Algorithms:** These models are trained on historical data to predict future spare parts demand.

1. **Unsupervised Learning:**
   - **Clustering Algorithms:** Segmenting spare parts based on demand patterns, which can inform more granular forecasting approaches.
2. **Deep Learning:**
   - **Recurrent Neural Networks (RNNs):** Effective for time series data, capturing trends and seasonality in demand for spare parts.
3. **Reinforcement Learning:**
   - Can be applied for dynamic inventory management, adapting to changing demand patterns in real time.

Benefits of Machine Learning in Spare Parts Forecasting

- **Improved Forecast Accuracy:** ML models can capture complex patterns and relationships in demand data, leading to more precise forecasts.
- **Reduced Inventory Costs:** Optimized inventory levels can minimize holding costs and reduce the risk of obsolescence.
- **Enhanced Operational Efficiency:** Timely availability of spare parts can reduce equipment downtime and improve overall productivity.
- **Data-Driven Decision-Making:** Leveraging data insights enables better planning and resource allocation.

Challenges and Considerations

1. **Data Quality:** Accurate and comprehensive data is essential for training effective ML models. This may require significant data cleaning and preprocessing.
2. **Integration with Existing Systems:** Implementing ML solutions must align with current inventory management and supply chain processes.
3. **Interpretability of Models:** Many ML models can be complex, making it essential to ensure stakeholders understand the forecasting outcomes.
4. **Adaptation to Changing Conditions:** The models must be adaptable to changes in operational conditions, such as fluctuations in demand due to market conditions or equipment upgrades.

5. **Collaboration Between Departments:** Effective forecasting requires collaboration between maintenance, procurement, and operational teams to align demand predictions with actual needs.

Conclusion

Machine learning has the potential to significantly enhance the forecasting of spare parts in the oil and gas industry. By leveraging advanced algorithms to analyze historical demand data and operational conditions, companies can optimize their inventory management practices, reduce costs, and improve operational efficiency. As the industry continues to evolve, ongoing collaboration between data scientists and domain experts will be key to maximizing the benefits of ML in spare parts forecasting.

Financial Risk Management Machine Learning

Machine learning (ML) is increasingly being utilized in financial risk management, providing advanced tools and methodologies to identify, assess, and mitigate risks. Here are some key applications, techniques, and considerations for using machine learning in this domain:

Key Applications

1. Credit Risk Assessment:
   - Predictive Modeling: Use ML algorithms to predict the likelihood of default based on historical data. Common models include logistic regression, decision trees, and ensemble methods.
   - Feature Engineering: Identify key indicators of creditworthiness, such as income, credit history, and economic conditions.
2. Market Risk Management:
   - Value at Risk (VaR): Use machine learning to improve VaR calculations by modeling asset price movements and correlations.
   - Stress Testing: Simulate extreme market conditions using ML to assess potential losses in adverse scenarios.

1. Fraud Detection:
   - Anomaly Detection: Implement unsupervised learning techniques to identify unusual transaction patterns that may indicate fraud.
   - Supervised Learning: Train classifiers on historical fraud data to predict future fraudulent activities.
2. Operational Risk Management:
   - Predictive Maintenance: Analyze data from operational processes to predict failures and mitigate risks before they occur.
   - Text Analytics: Use natural language processing (NLP) to analyze unstructured data, such as customer complaints or regulatory communications.
3. **Portfolio Management**:
   - **Asset Allocation**: Use ML algorithms to optimize portfolio allocations based on risk and return profiles.
   - **Sentiment Analysis**: Analyze news and social media sentiment to inform investment decisions.
4. Techniques

- **Supervised Learning**:
  - **Classification Algorithms**: Logistic regression, support vector machines, random forests, gradient boosting machines.
  - **Regression Algorithms**: Linear regression, polynomial regression, LSTM for time-series forecasting.
- **Unsupervised Learning**:
  - **Clustering**: K-means, hierarchical clustering for grouping similar risk profiles.
  - **Dimensionality Reduction**: PCA, t-SNE for feature selection and visualization.
- **Reinforcement Learning**:
  - Used in portfolio optimization and trading strategies to adaptively learn from the environment.
- **Deep Learning**:
  - Neural networks for complex pattern recognition in high-dimensional data, especially in fraud detection and sentiment analysis.

Considerations

1. **Data Quality**:
   - Ensure high-quality, clean, and relevant data for training models. Data preprocessing and cleaning are critical steps.
2. **Interpretability**:
   - Financial institutions often require transparency in decision-making. Use interpretable models or techniques like SHAP and LIME to explain model predictions.
3. **Regulatory Compliance**:
   - Adhere to financial regulations and standards. Ensure that ML models meet compliance requirements regarding fairness and accountability.
4. **Model Validation**:
   - Implement robust validation techniques, such as cross-validation and back testing, to assess model performance.
5. **Ethical Considerations**:
   - Be mindful of biases in data and models that could lead to unfair treatment of certain groups, especially in credit scoring.

Conclusion

Machine learning offers powerful tools for financial risk management, enabling organizations to enhance their risk assessment and mitigation strategies. However, successful implementation requires careful consideration of data quality, model interpretability, compliance, and ethical implications. As the field evolves, ongoing research and collaboration between data scientists and financial experts will be crucial for unlocking the full potential of ML in this area.

Stock market research Machine Learning

Machine learning (ML) has become an invaluable tool for stock market research, enabling analysts and traders to make data-driven decisions. Here's an overview of key applications, techniques, and considerations for using machine learning in this field.

Key Applications

1. **Price Prediction**:
   - **Time Series Forecasting**: Use historical price data to predict future stock prices using models like ARIMA, LSTM, or GRU.
   - **Regression Models**: Apply regression techniques to identify relationships between stock prices and economic indicators.
2. **Sentiment Analysis**:
   - **News and Social Media**: Analyze sentiment from financial news articles and social media platforms (e.g., Twitter) to gauge market sentiment and its potential impact on stock prices.
   - **Natural Language Processing (NLP)**: Use NLP techniques to extract sentiment from unstructured text data.
3. **Algorithmic Trading**:
   - **Automated Trading Systems**: Develop algorithms that execute trades based on predefined criteria derived from ML models.

   - **Reinforcement Learning**: Implement RL techniques to develop adaptive trading strategies that learn from market conditions.
4. **Risk Management**:
   - **Portfolio Optimization**: Use ML algorithms to optimize asset allocation based on historical performance and risk tolerance.
   - **Value at Risk (VaR)**: Apply ML techniques to calculate and predict VaR, assessing potential losses in an investment portfolio.
5. **Anomaly Detection**:
   - Identify unusual trading patterns or price movements that may indicate market manipulation or fraud.
6. **Market Regime Detection**:
   - Classify different market regimes (bullish, bearish, sideways) and adjust trading strategies accordingly.

Techniques

1. **Supervised Learning**:
   - **Classification Algorithms**: Use algorithms like decision trees, random forests, and support vector machines (SVM) to classify stocks based on buy/sell signals.
   - **Regression Analysis**: Employ linear regression, ridge regression, or ensemble methods to predict stock prices.
2. **Unsupervised Learning**:
   - **Clustering**: Group stocks with similar behaviors or performance metrics to identify trends and investment opportunities.
   - **Dimensionality Reduction**: Use techniques like PCA to reduce the complexity of financial datasets.
3. **Deep Learning**:
   - **Neural Networks**: Implement feedforward neural networks or convolutional neural networks (CNNs) for more complex pattern recognition.
   - **LSTM Networks**: Utilize LSTM for time series predictions to capture long-term dependencies in stock price movements.
4. **Natural Language Processing (NLP)**:
   - Use sentiment analysis and topic modeling to analyze financial news and social media data.

5. **Reinforcement Learning**:
   - Develop trading strategies that adapt based on market feedback and performance.

Considerations

1. **Data Quality**:
   - High-quality, clean, and relevant data is essential. Ensure data sources are reliable and perform thorough preprocessing.
2. **Feature Engineering**:
   - Carefully select and engineer features that capture relevant market dynamics and trends.
3. **Model Interpretability**:
   - Use interpretable models or techniques to explain predictions, particularly important for stakeholders in financial contexts.
4. **Backtesting**:
   - Implement robust backtesting to evaluate model performance on historical data before deploying in live trading.
5. **Risk Management**:
   - Incorporate risk management strategies into ML models to mitigate potential losses.
6. **Regulatory Compliance**:
   - Ensure adherence to financial regulations and standards, mainly when using customer data or implementing automated trading strategies.

Conclusion

Machine learning offers powerful tools for stock market research, enabling analysts to uncover patterns, optimize trading strategies, and make informed decisions. However, successful implementation requires careful consideration of data quality, model selection, and risk management. As technology evolves, ongoing research and adaptation will be crucial to stay ahead in the dynamic financial markets.

GAN-Based Market Simulation for Derivatives Pricing and Dynamic Hedging

Generative Adversarial Networks (GANs) have emerged as a powerful tool in various fields, including finance. They can be used for market simulation, providing synthetic data for derivatives pricing and dynamic hedging strategies. This approach allows financial institutions to model complex market behaviors and improve risk management.

Key Concepts

1. **Generative Adversarial Networks (GANs):**
    - A type of machine learning framework where two neural networks, the generator and the discriminator, are trained simultaneously.
    - The generator creates synthetic data, while the discriminator evaluates the authenticity of the generated data compared to real data.
2. **Derivatives Pricing:**
    - The process of determining the fair value of financial derivatives, such as options and futures.
    - Traditional models (e.g., Black-Scholes) may not capture the complexities of real market dynamics.
3. **Dynamic Hedging:**
    - A strategy that involves adjusting the hedge position as market conditions change to manage risk effectively.

  - Requires continuous monitoring of market conditions and recalibration of positions.

Applications

1. **Market Simulation:**
   - GANs can generate realistic market data, including prices, volumes, and volatility patterns.
   - Synthetic data can help in stress testing, scenario analysis, and exploring the impact of different market conditions on derivatives.
2. **Pricing Derivatives:**
   - By simulating various market scenarios, GANs can provide insights into the potential future prices of underlying assets, improving the accuracy of derivative pricing models.
   - The generated data can be used to train other models (e.g., neural networks) for pricing options and other derivatives.
3. **Dynamic Hedging Strategies:**
   - GAN-generated market scenarios can inform the development of hedging strategies that adapt to changing market conditions.
   - Using reinforcement learning in conjunction with GANs can optimize hedging decisions based on simulated market environments.

Techniques Used

1. **GAN Architecture:**
   - **Generator:** Produces synthetic market data based on noise input, aiming to mimic the statistical properties of real market data.
   - **Discriminator:** Evaluates the authenticity of the generated data, learning to distinguish between real and synthetic data.
2. **Conditional GANs (cGANs):**
   - These extend GANs by conditioning the generation process on specific variables (e.g., time, market conditions) to produce more relevant market scenarios.
3. **Reinforcement Learning:**
   - Can be integrated with GANs to optimize trading strategies and dynamic hedging based on simulated market outcomes.

4. **Data Augmentation:**
   - GANs can create additional training data for traditional pricing models, improving their robustness and accuracy.

Benefits

1. **Realistic Market Data Generation:**
   - GANs can capture complex dependencies and distributions present in financial markets, producing more realistic data than traditional models.
2. **Enhanced Risk Management:**
   - Financial institutions can better understand potential risks and devise more effective hedging strategies by simulating a wide range of market scenarios.
3. **Improved Pricing Accuracy:**
   - Synthetic data can lead to more informed pricing decisions, helping to avoid underpricing or overpricing derivatives.
4. **Cost Efficiency:**
   - Reduces the need for expensive data acquisition processes by generating synthetic datasets for analysis and model training.

Challenges and Considerations

1. **Model Training:**
   - Training GANs can be challenging due to issues like mode collapse (where the generator produces limited outputs) and stability in training.
2. **Interpretability:**
   - The "black box" nature of GANs can make it challenging to understand the underlying factors driving generated market behaviors.
3. **Regulatory Compliance:**
   - Financial institutions must ensure that synthetic data generation and usage comply with regulatory standards, especially concerning risk assessments.
4. **Quality of Synthetic Data:**
   - The generated data must be rigorously validated to ensure it reflects realistic market conditions and dynamics.

Conclusion

GAN-based market simulation offers a promising approach to derivatives pricing and dynamic hedging in finance. By generating realistic market data, these models enhance the understanding of market behaviors and improve risk management strategies. As research and technology continue to evolve, integrating GANs with other machine learning techniques will further optimize financial decision-making processes. Collaboration between data scientists and finance professionals will be essential to leverage these advancements effectively.

Consumer Credit Risk

Consumer credit risk assessment is critical for financial institutions to evaluate borrowers' likelihood of defaulting on their loans. Machine learning (ML) has become an invaluable tool in this field, enabling more accurate predictions and better risk management strategies.

Key Concepts

1. **Credit Risk Assessment:**
   - The process of determining the creditworthiness of potential borrowers based on various financial and demographic factors.
2. **Machine Learning Algorithms:**
   - Various algorithms are used to analyze historical data and predict credit risk, including logistic regression, decision trees, random forests, support vector machines, and neural networks.

Applications of Machine Learning in Credit Risk

1. **Predictive Modeling:**
   - ML algorithms can predict the likelihood of default by analyzing historical data on borrower behavior, repayment history, and other relevant factors.

- Common models include:
  - **Logistic Regression:** A baseline model for binary classification of default risk.
  - **Decision Trees and Random Forests:** Useful for handling non-linear relationships and interactions between features.
  - **Gradient Boosting Machines:** Effective for improving prediction accuracy through ensemble learning.
  - **Neural Networks:** Can capture complex patterns in large datasets, especially in deep learning architectures.

1. **Feature Engineering:**
   - Identifying and creating relevant features that improve model performance is crucial. Key features may include:
     - **Demographic Information:** Age, income, employment status, etc.
     - **Credit History:** Previous loans, payment history, outstanding debt.
     - **Behavioral Data:** Transaction patterns, spending habits.
2. **Risk Segmentation:**
   - Using clustering techniques (e.g., K-means) to identify groups of consumers with similar risk profiles helps tailor credit offerings and risk management strategies.
3. **Anomaly Detection:**
   - ML algorithms can detect unusual patterns in borrowing behavior that may indicate fraud or higher risk.
4. **Credit Scoring:**
   - Automating the ML credit scoring process can lead to more consistent and unbiased assessments, improving decision-making.

Techniques Used

1. **Supervised Learning:**
   - Most common approach for credit risk modeling, where historical data is used to train models to predict outcomes (e.g., default vs. non-default).
2. **Unsupervised Learning:**
   - Techniques like clustering can help identify distinct borrower segments, allowing for more personalized risk assessments.

1. **Reinforcement Learning:**
   - Can be employed to optimize lending strategies based on feedback from loan performance over time.
2. **Deep Learning:**
   - Neural networks, particularly recurrent neural networks (RNNs) and convolutional neural networks (CNNs), can analyze sequential data and complex relationships in large datasets.

Benefits of Machine Learning in Credit Risk

1. **Improved Prediction Accuracy:**
   - ML models can uncover intricate patterns and relationships in data that traditional statistical methods may miss, leading to better risk predictions.
2. **Efficiency and Speed:**
   - Automating the credit risk assessment process reduces the time taken to evaluate applications, leading to faster decision-making.
3. **Scalability:**
   - ML models can easily scale to handle large volumes of data from diverse sources, accommodating the growing demand for credit.
4. **Enhanced Decision-Making:**
   - By integrating ML insights, lenders can make more informed decisions, reducing default rates and optimizing portfolio performance.

Challenges and Considerations

1. **Data Quality:**
   - High-quality, comprehensive datasets are essential for effective model training. Incomplete or biased data can lead to poor predictions.
2. **Interpretability:**
   - Many ML models, especially complex ones like neural networks, can be difficult to interpret, making it challenging to explain decisions to stakeholders.

1. **Regulatory Compliance:**
   - Financial institutions must ensure that their models comply with regulatory standards, particularly regarding fairness, transparency, and accountability in lending practices.
2. **Bias and Fairness:**
   - ML models can inadvertently learn biases present in historical data, leading to unfair treatment of certain demographic groups. Ongoing monitoring and fairness assessments are essential.

Conclusion

Machine learning offers significant consumer credit risk assessment advancements, enabling more accurate predictions and improved risk management strategies. By leveraging these technologies, financial institutions can enhance their lending practices, reduce default rates, and better serve their customers. However, careful attention must be paid to data quality, model interpretability, and compliance to ensure responsible and ethical use of ML in this critical area.

Consumer Credit Analysis

Consumer credit analysis is essential for financial institutions to assess applicants' creditworthiness, manage risk, and make informed lending decisions. Machine learning (ML) techniques can significantly enhance the accuracy and efficiency of credit analysis by analyzing vast amounts of data and identifying patterns that traditional methods may overlook.

Key Objectives

1. **Credit Risk Assessment:** Determine the likelihood of default on loans or credit cards.
2. **Fraud Detection:** Identify potentially fraudulent activities in credit applications.
3. **Customer Segmentation:** Classify customers into different risk profiles for tailored marketing and risk management strategies.

Data Sources

- **Demographic Data:** Age, income, employment status, education level, etc.
- **Credit History:** Previous loans, repayment history, credit utilization ratio, and credit score.
- **Transaction Data:** Spending patterns, payment behavior, and account balances.

- **Macroeconomic Indicators:** Economic conditions that may influence credit risk, such as unemployment rates and inflation.

Applications of Machine Learning

1. **Predictive Modeling:**
    - **Classification Algorithms:**
        - **Logistic Regression:** A baseline model to predict the probability of default.
        - **Decision Trees and Random Forests:** Capture non-linear relationships and interactions between features.
        - **Gradient Boosting Machines (GBM):** Effective for handling imbalanced datasets common in credit analysis.
    - **Neural Networks:** Can model complex relationships and interactions in high-dimensional data.
2. **Risk Scoring:**
    - ML models can assign risk scores to applicants based on their profiles, helping lenders decide on loan approvals and terms.
3. **Fraud Detection:**
    - **Anomaly Detection Algorithms:** Identify unusual patterns in transaction data that may indicate fraud.
    - **Supervised Learning Models:** Train on historical fraud cases to predict and flag potential fraud in new applications.
4. **Customer Segmentation:**
    - **Clustering Techniques:** Use algorithms like K-means or hierarchical clustering to group consumers based on credit risk profiles, allowing for targeted marketing and risk management strategies.

Techniques Used

1. **Supervised Learning:**
    - **Classification Techniques:** Logistic regression, support vector machines, decision trees, and ensemble methods for predicting defaults.
    - **Regression Techniques:** Predicting continuous outcomes such as credit scores or loan amounts.
2. **Unsupervised Learning:**
    - **Clustering Algorithms:** Segmenting customers into different risk groups without predefined labels.

- **Dimensionality Reduction:** Techniques like PCA to reduce feature space and highlight important variables.

3. **Deep Learning:**
    - **Neural Networks:** Effective for processing large datasets with complex relationships, beneficial for feature extraction in high-dimensional data.
4. **Reinforcement Learning:**
    - Can be applied in adaptive credit scoring models that learn from new data and evolving economic conditions.

Benefits of Machine Learning in Consumer Credit Analysis

- **Improved Accuracy:** ML models can identify subtle patterns in data that enhance the accuracy of credit risk assessments.
- **Faster Decision-Making:** Automation of the analysis process allows for quicker loan approvals and more efficient credit management.
- **Enhanced Fraud Detection:** ML algorithms can quickly analyze transaction data and flag potential fraud in real-time.
- **Personalization:** Tailored credit offers and risk management strategies based on individual customer profiles.

Challenges and Considerations

1. **Data Quality:** High-quality, representative datasets are essential for training effective models. Data preprocessing, cleaning, and feature engineering are critical steps.
2. **Interpretability:** Many ML models, especially deep learning, can be complex and challenging to interpret. Ensuring that stakeholders understand model decisions is important for trust and compliance.
3. **Regulatory Compliance:** Financial institutions must ensure that their models comply with regulations regarding fairness and transparency, particularly in lending decisions.
4. **Bias and Fairness:** Addressing biases in training data is crucial to prevent discrimination against certain groups, especially in sensitive applications like credit scoring.
5. **Integration into Existing Systems:** Implementing ML solutions requires careful integration into current credit analysis workflows and systems.

Conclusion

Machine learning offers powerful tools for enhancing consumer credit analysis, leading to improved risk assessment, faster decision-making, and more personalized customer interactions. By leveraging advanced algorithms to analyze complex data, financial institutions can better manage credit risk and respond to their customers' evolving needs. Ongoing collaboration between data scientists and credit analysts will be essential to refining these models and ensuring their successful application in real-world scenarios.

Occupations and the Economy

Machine learning (ML) is increasingly being utilized to analyze the relationships between occupations and economic factors. Researchers and businesses can gain insights into labor market trends, skill demands, wage predictions, and economic forecasts by leveraging large datasets and advanced algorithms. Here's an overview of how ML can be applied in this context.

Key Applications

1. **Labor Market Analysis**:
   - **Job Market Trends**: Analyzing job postings and hiring data to identify trends in demand for specific occupations.
   - **Skill Gap Analysis**: Using ML to compare required skills in job descriptions with available workforce skills to identify gaps.
2. **Wage Prediction**:
   - **Salary Estimation**: Predicting wages based on factors such as occupation, education level, location, and industry using regression models.
   - **Income Disparity Analysis**: Understanding wage disparities across different occupations and demographics.
3. **Occupational Classification**:

- **Automated Job Classification**: Using natural language processing (NLP) to categorize job descriptions into standardized occupational classifications (e.g., O*NET).
- **Clustering Occupations**: Identifying similar occupations based on required skills, responsibilities, and market demand.

4. **Economic Forecasting**:
    - **Predicting Economic Outcomes**: Applying time series forecasting to predict the impact of job market changes on local and national economies.
    - **Analyzing Economic Indicators**: Using ML to analyze how shifts in employment rates affect GDP, inflation, and other economic indicators.
5. **Workforce Development**:
    - **Training Program Effectiveness**: Evaluating the impact of educational programs and training on employment outcomes using causal inference techniques.
    - **Career Pathways Analysis**: Mapping potential career trajectories based on current occupations and skill sets.
6. **Unemployment Prediction**:
    - **Risk Assessment**: Identifying individuals or demographics at higher risk of unemployment using classification algorithms.
    - **Job Retention Analysis**: Understanding factors that contribute to job retention and turnover through survival analysis.

Techniques Used

1. **Supervised Learning**:
    - **Regression Models**: For predicting wages and economic outcomes based on various features.
    - **Classification Models**: For predicting job categories or employment status.
2. **Unsupervised Learning**:
    - **Clustering**: K-means or hierarchical clustering to identify groups of similar occupations or skills.
    - **Dimensionality Reduction**: Techniques like PCA to reduce complexity in feature sets.

1. **Natural Language Processing (NLP)**:
    - **Text Mining**: Analyzing job descriptions and resumes to extract relevant features and insights.
    - **Sentiment Analysis**: Assessing public sentiment toward different occupations or industries based on social media data.
2. **Time Series Analysis**:
    - **Forecasting Models**: ARIMA, LSTM, and other models to predict future job market trends based on historical data.
3. **Reinforcement Learning**:
    - **Dynamic Workforce Planning**: Developing adaptive strategies for workforce management and training.

Benefits of Using Machine Learning

- **Data-Driven Insights**: ML allows for the analysis of large volumes of data, revealing patterns and insights that traditional methods may overlook.
- **Informed Decision-Making**: Businesses and policymakers can make better decisions regarding hiring, training, and economic policies based on predictive models.
- **Enhanced Efficiency**: Automating tasks like job classification and wage prediction reduces manual effort and increases accuracy.

Challenges and Considerations

1. **Data Quality**: High-quality, comprehensive data is crucial for effective ML applications. Inaccurate or biased data can lead to flawed models.
2. **Interpretability**: Many ML models, especially deep learning models, can act as "black boxes," making it challenging to understand decision-making processes.
3. **Ethical Implications**: Care must be taken to avoid reinforcing biases in hiring and promotions based on flawed algorithms.
4. **Dynamic Labor Market**: The rapidly changing nature of work requires continuous model updates to remain relevant.

Conclusion

Machine learning offers powerful tools for analyzing the relationships between occupations and the economy. Organizations can gain valuable insights into labor market trends, wage dynamics, and workforce development strategies by leveraging ML techniques. As the job market continues to evolve, the integration of ML in economic analysis will play a critical role in shaping effective policies and practices. Ongoing collaboration between data scientists, economists, and industry experts will be essential to maximize the benefits of ML in this field.

Comparison and Financial Assessment of Demand Forecasting Methodologies for Seasonal Consumer Packaged Goods (CPGs)

Demand forecasting is critical for managing inventory and optimizing supply chains, especially for seasonal Consumer Packaged Goods (CPGs). Machine learning (ML) methodologies offer advanced techniques for improving demand predictions. This overview compares various ML methods and assesses their financial implications for seasonal CPGs.

Key Demand Forecasting Methodologies

1. **Time Series Analysis**:
    - **ARIMA (Auto Regressive Integrated Moving Average)**: A classic statistical method suitable for time series data. It effectively captures seasonality and trends.
    - **Seasonal Decomposition of Time Series (STL)**: Decomposes time series into seasonal, trend, and residual components for improved forecasting.
2. **Machine Learning Approaches**:
    - **Regression Models**:
        - **Linear Regression**: Simple but effective for capturing linear relationships.
        - **Polynomial Regression**: Captures non-linear trends in demand.

- **Tree-Based Models**:
  - **Random Forest**: An ensemble method that improves prediction accuracy by aggregating multiple decision trees.
  - **Gradient Boosting Machines (GBM)**: Focuses on minimizing errors by sequentially improving weak models.
- **Deep Learning**:
  - **Recurrent Neural Networks (RNNs)**: Particularly effective for sequential data; captures long-term dependencies.
  - **Long Short-Term Memory (LSTM)**: A type of RNN that addresses vanishing gradient issues, making it suitable for longer sequences.

1. **Hybrid Models**:
   - **Combining Statistical and ML Methods**: Utilizing ARIMA for trend extraction and ML models for residual error modeling to enhance accuracy.

Comparison of Methodologies

Methodology	Strengths	Weaknesses	Best Use Case
ARIMA	Good for univariate time series	Assumes linearity, limited to past data	Short-term forecasts with clear seasonality
Linear Regression	Easy to implement and interpret	Struggles with non-linear patterns	Simple demand relationships
Random Forest	Handles non-linear relationships well	Requires large datasets	Complex relationships with multiple features
LSTM	Captures long-term dependencies	High computational cost	Sequential demand data
Hybrid Models	Combines strengths of multiple approaches	Complexity in implementation	Data with both trends and seasonal effects

Financial Assessment

1. **Cost Savings**:
   - Accurate demand forecasts reduce excess inventory and associated holding costs, leading to significant cost savings.
   - Lower stockouts improve customer satisfaction, leading to higher sales and customer retention.
2. **Revenue Optimization**:
   - Better forecasting allows for strategic pricing and promotions, optimizing revenue during peak seasons.

    - Accurate demand predictions enable businesses to take advantage of economies of scale, reducing per-unit costs.
3. **Risk Mitigation**:
    - Effective forecasting reduces risks associated with overproduction or underproduction, stabilizing cash flows.
    - Understanding seasonal demand patterns can inform strategic decisions related to capacity planning and resource allocation.
4. **Investment in Technology**:
    - While implementing advanced ML models may require upfront investment in technology and talent, the long-term benefits often outweigh these costs.
    - Continuous improvement through model updates and refinements leads to better financial outcomes.

Case Study Example

- **Company X**: A seasonal CPG manufacturer implemented LSTM models and compared them with traditional ARIMA forecasts.
    - **Results**: Achieved a 15% reduction in forecast error compared to ARIMA.
    - **Financial Impact**: Reduced inventory holding costs by 20% during peak season, leading to an additional $2 million in revenue.

Conclusion

Machine learning methodologies for demand forecasting in seasonal CPGs offer significant accuracy and financial performance advantages. Organizations can select the most suitable methods by comparing various approaches based on their specific needs and capabilities. Implementing these advanced techniques can lead to substantial cost savings, improved revenue management, and enhanced risk mitigation, ultimately driving greater profitability in a competitive market.

Insurance Claims Machine Learning

Using machine learning (ML) to detect and prevent insurance claim fraud is an increasingly important area within the insurance industry. ML techniques can analyze large volumes of data to identify patterns and anomalies that may indicate fraudulent activities. Here's an overview of key applications, techniques, and considerations for applying ML to insurance claim fraud detection.

Key Applications

1. **Fraud Detection**:
   - **Anomaly Detection**: Identify unusual patterns in claims data that deviate from the norm, potentially indicating fraudulent behavior.
   - **Pattern Recognition**: Detect common fraud patterns, such as false claims, exaggerated damages, or collusion among claimants.
2. **Risk Scoring**:
   - Assign risk scores to claims based on various features, helping insurance adjusters prioritize investigations on high-risk claims.
3. **Automated Claims Processing**:
   - Streamline the claims process by automatically flagging suspicious claims for further review, reducing manual workload.

4. **Customer Profiling**:
   - Analyze historical data to profile typical claimants and flag claims that fall outside of established profiles.
5. **Real-Time Monitoring**:
   - Implement systems that monitor claims in real time, allowing for immediate investigation of suspicious claims.

Techniques

1. **Supervised Learning**:
   - **Classification Algorithms**: Based on labeled training data, use algorithms like logistic regression, decision trees, random forests, and support vector machines (SVM) to classify claims as legitimate or fraudulent.
   - **Ensemble Methods**: Combine multiple models to improve prediction accuracy and robustness, such as using random forests or gradient boosting.
2. **Unsupervised Learning**:
   - **Clustering**: Group similar claims to identify outliers that may indicate fraud. Techniques like K-means or DBSCAN can be useful for this purpose.
   - **Anomaly Detection**: Implement methods like isolation forests or one-class SVMs to detect anomalous claims without labeled data.
3. **Natural Language Processing (NLP)**:
   - Analyze text data from claims descriptions, customer communications, or social media to identify red flags or suspicious language patterns.
4. **Deep Learning**:
   - **Neural Networks**: Utilize deep learning models for complex pattern recognition, especially when dealing with unstructured data (e.g., images of damage).
   - **Recurrent Neural Networks (RNNs)**: Apply RNNs for sequence data, such as time series of claims submitted over time.
5. **Feature Engineering**:
   - Create features based on historical data, including frequency of claims, claim amounts, types of claims, and customer demographics.

Considerations

1. **Data Quality**:
   - Ensure high-quality data for training models. Data cleaning and preprocessing are critical to improving model performance.
2. **Interpretability**:
   - Use interpretable models or techniques (e.g., SHAP values) to explain model predictions, which is important for gaining trust from stakeholders.
3. **Regulatory Compliance**:
   - Adhere to regulations regarding data privacy and fair treatment of claimants. Ensure that models do not introduce bias against certain groups.
4. **Model Validation**:
   - Implement robust validation techniques, including cross-validation and backtesting, to assess model performance before deployment.
5. **Collaboration with Domain Experts**:
   - Work closely with insurance professionals to ensure that the models address relevant fraud scenarios and are grounded in industry knowledge.
6. **Scalability**:
   - Choose models and infrastructure that can scale as data volume increases, especially as more digital claims are processed.

Conclusion

Machine learning offers powerful tools for detecting and preventing insurance claim fraud, helping insurers save money and reduce losses. By leveraging data effectively and implementing robust ML techniques, insurance companies can enhance their fraud detection capabilities. Continuous monitoring and collaboration between data scientists and insurance experts will be essential to adapting to evolving fraud tactics and improving overall effectiveness in combating fraud.

Systems Theory Approach to Cybersecurity Using Supervised Machine Learning

Cybersecurity is a multifaceted domain that requires a comprehensive approach to protecting systems from threats. Systems theory provides a holistic framework for understanding complex interactions within cybersecurity environments. By integrating supervised machine learning (ML) techniques into this framework, organizations can enhance their ability to detect, prevent, and respond effectively to cyber threats.

1. Systems Theory Overview

- **Definition**: Systems theory studies complex systems and their interrelated components, focusing on how they operate as a whole.
- **Key Concepts**:
  - **Holism**: The idea that a system must be analyzed as a whole rather than through its individual components.
  - **Feedback Loops**: The processes through which outputs of a system are circled back as inputs, influencing future behavior.
  - **Emergent Properties**: Characteristics of a system that emerge from the interactions of its components, which cannot be understood by examining the components in isolation.

2. Application of Systems Theory in Cybersecurity

- **Holistic Security Architecture**: A systems approach encourages the integration of people, processes, and technology, creating a cohesive security posture.
- **Dynamic Risk Assessment**: By understanding feedback loops, organizations can continuously assess risks based on changing threat landscapes and system vulnerabilities.
- **Collaborative Defense**: Systems theory emphasizes the importance of cooperation among various stakeholders, including IT teams, management, and external partners, to strengthen security measures.

3. Supervised Machine Learning in Cybersecurity

Supervised machine learning involves training algorithms on labeled datasets to predict outcomes for new, unseen data. In cybersecurity, this can enhance threat detection and response.

- **Common Techniques**:
  - **Classification Algorithms**: Used to identify whether a given event or behavior is benign or malicious (e.g., decision trees, random forests, support vector machines).
  - **Regression Algorithms**: Useful for predicting the severity of a threat based on various features.
  - **Neural Networks**: Especially deep learning, which can analyze complex patterns in large datasets, such as network traffic.

4. Integrating Systems Theory with Supervised Machine Learning

- **Data Collection and Preparation**: Utilize systems thinking to identify critical data sources across the organization, ensuring comprehensive coverage of potential indicators of compromise.
- **Feature Engineering**: Leverage knowledge of system interactions to create relevant features for ML models. This might include:
  - User behavior analytics (UBA)
  - Network flow data

  - Endpoint metrics
- **Model Training**: Use labeled datasets to train models on historical cyber incidents. This includes defining:
  - **Positive Classes**: Malicious activities (e.g., malware infections, unauthorized access)
  - **Negative Classes**: Normal activities
- **Feedback Mechanisms**: Incorporate feedback loops into the training process:
  - Continuously retrain models with new data to adapt to evolving threats.
  - Use incident responses to refine model accuracy and improve predictions.

5. Implementation Steps

1. **Identify Key Systems**: Map out the critical assets and systems within the organization.
2. **Data Gathering**: Collect data from various sources, including logs, alerts, and historical incidents.
3. **Feature Selection**: Identify key features, such as IP addresses, user behavior, and access patterns, that contribute to predicting cyber threats.
4. **Model Selection and Training**: Based on the specific use case, choose appropriate supervised ML algorithms and train them using the prepared data.
5. **Deployment and Monitoring**: Implement the models in a real-time monitoring system to detect anomalies and threats. Set up dashboards for continuous assessment.
6. **Iterative Improvement**: Regularly evaluate model performance and update the training data and features based on new threats and feedback from security teams.

6. Challenges and Considerations

- **Data Quality**: Ensuring high-quality, relevant data is essential for effective model training.
- **Interpretability**: Many ML models can be complex, making it difficult for security teams to interpret results. Techniques like SHAP or LIME can help.

- **Integration with Existing Systems**: Aligning new ML models with existing security infrastructure requires careful planning.
- **Compliance and Privacy**: Ensure adherence to regulations regarding data privacy and security.

7. Conclusion

Integrating a systems theory approach with supervised machine learning enhances cybersecurity strategies by promoting a holistic understanding of complex interactions within systems. This combination allows organizations to develop proactive measures against cyber threats, leveraging data-driven insights to strengthen their security posture continuously. Ongoing collaboration among stakeholders and adaptation to evolving threats will be key to successful implementation.

Poisoning Cyberattacks

Poisoning attacks, particularly in the context of machine learning (ML), involve the intentional manipulation of training data to degrade the performance of ML models. As organizations increasingly rely on ML systems for security and decision-making, understanding how poisoning attacks work and developing defenses against them has become crucial.

1. Types of Poisoning Attacks

- **Data Poisoning**: Adversaries inject malicious data into the training set, causing the model to learn incorrect patterns.
  - **Label Flipping**: Changing the labels of a subset of training data to mislead the model.
  - **Backdoor Attacks**: Introducing specific data points that trigger malicious behavior when presented during inference.
- **Model Poisoning**: In collaborative or federated learning settings, attackers can manipulate model updates sent from compromised clients to the central server.

2. Mechanisms of Poisoning Attacks

- **Targeted Attacks**: Aim to misclassify specific instances or achieve a specific outcome. For example, altering training data so

that a face recognition model fails to recognize a certain individual.
- **Untargeted Attacks**: General degradation of model performance across multiple classes or instances without a specific target.

3. Machine Learning Techniques in Poisoning Attacks

- **Generative Models**: Adversaries can use generative models (like GANs) to create realistic-looking but malicious training data.
- **Gradient Descent Manipulation**: By understanding the training process, attackers can craft inputs that will significantly influence the model's weights during optimization.
- **Transfer Learning**: Utilizing a pre-trained model and injecting poisoned data that targets its learned representations.

4. Impact of Poisoning Attacks

- **Decreased Model Accuracy**: Models can misclassify inputs, leading to wrong decisions in critical applications such as finance or healthcare.
- **Loss of Trust**: Persistent poisoning attacks can erode trust in automated systems, affecting user confidence and compliance.
- **Financial Loss**: Organizations can suffer significant financial repercussions due to erroneous predictions or actions taken based on compromised models.

5. Detection and Mitigation Strategies

- **Data Validation**: Implementing robust data validation techniques to identify and reject potentially poisoned inputs before they are included in the training set.
- **Anomaly Detection**: Using ML models to detect unusual patterns in training data that may indicate poisoning.
- **Robust Training Methods**: Employing techniques like adversarial training or differential privacy to enhance the resilience of models against poisoning.
- **Regular Audits**: Conducting regular audits of training data and model performance to identify signs of degradation or bias introduced by poisoning.

- **Model Ensembling**: Combining predictions from multiple models trained on different data subsets can reduce the impact of a single poisoned model.

6. Future Directions

As ML systems become more prevalent in critical applications, the threat of poisoning attacks will likely increase. Ongoing research is necessary to develop more sophisticated detection and defense mechanisms. Collaboration between cybersecurity experts and machine learning practitioners will be essential to create robust systems capable of resisting such threats.

7. Conclusion

Poisoning attacks pose a significant threat to the integrity and reliability of machine learning systems. Organizations can better protect their systems against malicious interference and maintain trust in their automated decision-making processes by understanding the mechanisms behind these attacks and implementing effective detection and mitigation strategies.

Sales and Customer Segmentation Using Machine Learning

Customer segmentation is a crucial aspect of sales and marketing strategies, enabling businesses to tailor their offerings and optimize customer engagement. Machine learning (ML) enhances traditional segmentation methods by leveraging data to uncover hidden patterns and insights.

Key Applications of Machine Learning in Customer Segmentation

1. **Segmentation of Customer Base**:
   - **Behavioral Segmentation**: Identifying groups based on customer behaviors, such as purchase history, website interactions, and engagement levels.
   - **Demographic Segmentation**: Classifying customers based on age, gender, income, and location to tailor marketing strategies.
2. **Predictive Analytics**:
   - **Churn Prediction**: Using ML models to predict which customers are likely to stop purchasing, allowing proactive retention strategies.
   - **Customer Lifetime Value (CLV)**: Estimating the total revenue a customer will generate over their lifetime to prioritize high-value segments.

1. **Personalization**:
   - Tailoring recommendations and marketing messages to specific segments based on identified preferences and behaviors.
2. **Targeted Campaigns**:
   - Designing marketing campaigns aimed at specific segments, increasing the relevance and effectiveness of promotions.

Techniques Used in Customer Segmentation

1. **Clustering Algorithms**:
   - **K-Means**: A popular algorithm for partitioning customers into kkk distinct segments based on feature similarity.
   - **Hierarchical Clustering**: Builds a cluster tree, helping visualize relationships between different customer segments.
   - **DBSCAN**: Identifies clusters based on density, useful for detecting outliers in customer behavior.
2. **Dimensionality Reduction**:
   - **PCA (Principal Component Analysis)**: Reduces the dimensionality of data while preserving variance, making clustering more efficient.
   - **t-SNE**: A technique for visualizing high-dimensional data, aiding in understanding customer segments.
3. **Supervised Learning**:
   - **Classification Models**: After segmentation, models like decision trees or random forests can classify new customers into existing segments based on their features.
4. **Regression Models**:
   - Used for predicting metrics like CLV or estimating the impact of marketing strategies on different segments.
5. **Natural Language Processing (NLP)**:
   - Analyzing customer feedback, reviews, and social media interactions to understand sentiments and trends.

Implementation Steps

1. **Data Collection**: Gather data from various sources, including CRM systems, sales databases, and web analytics.
2. **Data Preprocessing**: Clean and normalize data, handle missing values, and encode categorical variables.

3. **Feature Selection**: Identify relevant features that will help in meaningful segmentation.
4. **Model Selection**: Choose appropriate ML algorithms for clustering or classification based on the nature of the data.
5. **Model Training and Evaluation**: Train the model on historical data and evaluate its performance using metrics such as silhouette score for clustering.
6. **Deployment and Monitoring**: Implement the model in a production environment, continuously monitor its performance, and adjust as necessary.

Benefits of Using Machine Learning for Customer Segmentation

- **Improved Accuracy**: ML can uncover complex patterns in data that traditional methods might miss, leading to more precise segmentation.
- **Dynamic Segmentation**: ML models can adapt to changes in customer behavior and preferences over time.
- **Enhanced Personalization**: By understanding customer segments deeply, businesses can offer more relevant products and services.
- **Resource Optimization**: Targeted campaigns ensure marketing resources are used more efficiently, maximizing return on investment.

Conclusion

Machine learning significantly enhances the ability to segment customers effectively, allowing businesses to make data-driven decisions that improve marketing effectiveness and customer satisfaction. By leveraging advanced techniques, organizations can better understand their customers, predict future behaviors, and tailor their strategies to meet diverse needs.

Invoice-to-Cash Collection Through Machine Learning

The Invoice-to-Cash (I2C) process is a critical component of business financial management, encompassing all activities from invoicing customers to collecting payments. Machine learning can significantly enhance this process by optimizing cash collection strategies, predicting payment behaviors, and automating various tasks. Here's an overview of how machine learning can be applied to the I2C process.

Key Applications of Machine Learning in I2C

1. **Payment Prediction**:
    - **Predictive Analytics**: Use historical data to predict when a customer is likely to pay an invoice. Machine learning models can analyze patterns in payment history to forecast payment timing and amounts.
2. **Risk Assessment**:
    - **Credit Scoring**: Develop models to assess customers' creditworthiness based on historical payment behavior, financial stability, and other relevant features.
3. **Customer Segmentation**:
    - **Segmentation for Targeted Follow-Ups**: Use clustering algorithms to segment customers based on their payment behaviors, allowing for tailored follow-up strategies.

1. **Churn Prediction**:
    - **Identifying At-Risk Customers**: Predict which customers are likely to delay payments or stop purchasing entirely. This enables proactive outreach to address issues before they lead to defaults.

2. **Automated Invoice Processing**:
    - **Natural Language Processing (NLP)**: Use NLP techniques to extract relevant information from invoices, improving data accuracy and reducing manual entry errors.
3. **Collection Strategy Optimization**:
    - **Dynamic Collection Strategies**: Use reinforcement learning to develop adaptive strategies for contacting customers based on their payment behaviors, optimizing the timing and method of outreach.

Techniques Used

1. **Supervised Learning**:
    - **Regression Models**: Predict payment amounts and timings using historical payment data.
    - **Classification Models**: Classify customers as high-risk or low-risk based on their payment histories.
2. **Unsupervised Learning**:
    - **Clustering**: Group customers into segments based on their payment behavior to tailor strategies accordingly.
3. **Time Series Analysis**:
    - **Forecasting**: Use time series models to predict future cash flows based on past payment trends.
4. **Natural Language Processing (NLP)**:
    - Automate the extraction of information from invoices and communications, facilitating better data management.

Implementation Steps

1. **Data Collection**:
    - Gather historical data, including invoices, payment history, customer communications, and external financial data.

2. **Data Preprocessing**:
    - Clean and normalize the data, handle missing values, and ensure consistency in the data format.
3. **Feature Engineering**:
    - Create relevant features that might influence payment behavior, such as invoice amount, due date, customer segment, and payment history.
4. **Model Selection**:
    - Choose appropriate machine learning models based on the problem type (regression for payment prediction, classification for risk assessment).
5. **Training and Evaluation**:
    - Train models using historical data and evaluate performance with metrics like accuracy, precision, recall, and mean absolute error.
6. **Deployment**:
    - Integrate the trained models into the existing invoicing and payment systems, ensuring that they can provide real-time insights and predictions.
7. **Monitoring and Maintenance**:
    - Continuously monitor model performance and retrain with new data to keep predictions accurate and relevant.

Benefits of Machine Learning in I2C

- **Increased Efficiency**: Automating tasks reduces the workload on finance teams and speeds up the invoicing process.
- **Improved Cash Flow**: Predictive insights enable proactive collection strategies, leading to faster payments and improved cash flow.
- **Better Decision-Making**: Data-driven insights enhance decision-making regarding credit limits, payment terms, and customer engagement strategies.
- **Reduced Churn**: Identifying at-risk customers allows for timely interventions, potentially reducing churn rates.

Conclusion

Implementing machine learning in the Invoice-to-Cash process can streamline operations, enhance decision-making, and ultimately improve cash flow for businesses. By leveraging predictive analytics, risk assessment, and automation, organizations can create a more efficient and responsive I2C process that meets the demands of today's fast-paced business environment.

Neural networks to understand intricate patterns of human interaction

Neural networks are a fascinating and complex area of research that can be used to understand intricate patterns of human interaction. Here's an overview of how neural networks can be applied, the types of data involved, and key techniques for analyzing human interactions.

Key Applications

1. **Social Network Analysis**:
   - **Community Detection**: Identify groups of individuals within social networks based on interaction patterns using techniques like graph neural networks.
   - **Influence Prediction**: Predict how information spreads through social networks by modeling interactions between users.
2. **Natural Language Processing (NLP)**:
   - **Sentiment Analysis**: Analyze textual data from social media, reviews, or conversations to gauge sentiments and emotions within human interactions.
   - **Chatbots and Conversational Agents**: Use recurrent neural networks (RNNs) or transformers to understand and generate human-like responses in dialogues.
3. **Video and Image Analysis**:

- **Facial Expression Recognition**: Apply convolutional neural networks (CNNs) to detect and interpret human emotions through facial expressions in images and videos.
- **Action Recognition**: Identify and classify human actions in videos, useful for understanding social dynamics in various settings.

4. **Human Activity Recognition**:
   - **Sensor Data**: Analyze data from wearable sensors to understand physical interactions and social behaviors in real-world environments.
   - **Contextual Understanding**: Combine data from multiple sources (e.g., GPS, accelerometers) to infer social interactions in specific contexts.
5. **Emotion Recognition**:
   - Use neural networks to analyze voice patterns, facial expressions, and body language to infer emotional states during interactions.
6. **Predictive Modeling**:
   - **Interaction Outcomes**: Predict outcomes of interactions (e.g., successful negotiations, relationship dynamics) based on historical interaction data.

Techniques

1. **Convolutional Neural Networks (CNNs)**:
   - Effective for processing spatial data, such as images of facial expressions or scenes depicting human interactions.
2. **Recurrent Neural Networks (RNNs)**:
   - Suitable for sequence data, such as dialogues in conversations. Long Short-Term Memory (LSTM) networks can capture long-range dependencies in dialogue contexts.
3. **Transformers**:
   - Highly effective for NLP tasks, enabling the analysis of textual data with attention mechanisms that capture relationships across different parts of input sequences.
4. **Graph Neural Networks (GNNs)**:
   - Useful for modeling relationships and interactions in social networks, capturing the complex interdependencies between individuals.

1. **Multimodal Learning**:
   - Combine various data types (text, audio, video) to gain a comprehensive understanding of human interactions. This involves training models that can process and integrate different modalities.

Considerations

1. **Data Privacy and Ethics**:
   - Respect individuals' privacy when collecting and analyzing interaction data. Ensure compliance with data protection regulations.
2. **Bias and Fairness**:
   - Be aware of potential biases in training data that can affect model performance and decision-making. Implement strategies to mitigate bias.
3. **Interpretability**:
   - Neural networks, especially deep learning models, can be complex and difficult to interpret. Use techniques like SHAP or LIME to explain model predictions.
4. **Scalability**:
   - Ensure that models can scale to handle large datasets, especially in real-time applications such as social media monitoring.
5. **Collaboration Across Disciplines**:
   - Work with sociology, psychology, and human behavior experts to ensure models are grounded in relevant theories and frameworks.

Conclusion

Neural networks offer powerful tools for understanding the intricate patterns of human interaction, enabling insights into social dynamics, emotional states, and communication patterns. By leveraging various data types and advanced modeling techniques, researchers and practitioners can gain a deeper understanding of human behavior and improve applications ranging from social media analysis to customer engagement strategies. Ongoing research and collaboration will be key to unlocking the full potential of neural networks in this domain.

Medical Science Machine Learning

Machine learning (ML) is making significant strides in medical science. It is transforming various aspects of healthcare, from diagnostics and treatment to personalized medicine and operational efficiency. Here's an overview of key applications, techniques, and considerations for using ML in medical science.

Key Applications

1. **Disease Diagnosis**:
    - **Medical Imaging**: Use deep learning algorithms to analyze medical images (e.g., X-rays, MRIs, CT scans) for conditions like tumors, fractures, or abnormalities.
    - **Pathology**: Automate the analysis of tissue samples to detect cancer or other diseases through image recognition.
2. **Predictive Analytics**:
    - **Risk Prediction**: Predict patient outcomes, such as the likelihood of developing chronic diseases (e.g., diabetes, heart disease) based on historical health data.
    - **Readmission Prediction**: Identify patients at risk of readmission to the hospital, enabling preventive measures to reduce healthcare costs.

1. **Personalized Medicine**:
   - **Treatment Recommendations**: Analyze genetic and clinical data to tailor treatment plans for individual patients, optimizing efficacy and minimizing side effects.
   - **Drug Discovery**: Use ML to identify potential drug candidates and predict their efficacy based on biological data.
2. **Natural Language Processing (NLP)**:
   - **Clinical Text Analysis**: Extract insights from clinical notes, research papers, and electronic health records (EHRs) to enhance decision-making and research.
   - **Chatbots and Virtual Assistants**: Implement NLP-powered chatbots to assist with patient inquiries and triage.
3. **Remote Monitoring and Wearables**:
   - **Patient Monitoring**: Analyze data from wearable devices to monitor vital signs and detect anomalies in real-time.
   - **Chronic Disease Management**: Use ML to provide insights and alerts for patients with chronic conditions, improving their management.
4. **Operational Efficiency**:
   - **Resource Optimization**: Analyze patient flow and operational data to optimize scheduling, staffing, and resource allocation in healthcare facilities.
   - **Fraud Detection**: Identify fraudulent claims and billing practices by analyzing patterns in healthcare data.

Techniques

1. **Supervised Learning**:
   - **Classification Algorithms**: Use models like logistic regression, decision trees, and support vector machines for tasks such as diagnosing diseases based on patient data.
   - **Regression Models**: Apply regression techniques to predict health outcomes based on various clinical features.
2. **Unsupervised Learning**:
   - **Clustering**: Group similar patient profiles to identify subpopulations that may benefit from targeted treatments.
   - **Dimensionality Reduction**: Use techniques like PCA to reduce the complexity of genomic data for analysis.

1. **Deep Learning**:
    - **Convolutional Neural Networks (CNNs)**: Utilize CNNs for image analysis tasks, such as interpreting medical scans or pathology slides.
    - **Recurrent Neural Networks (RNNs)**: Apply RNNs to analyze time-series data from patient monitoring systems.
2. **Reinforcement Learning**:
    - Use RL for treatment optimization, where models learn to recommend treatment plans based on patient responses over time.
3. **Natural Language Processing (NLP)**:
    - Implement NLP techniques for processing and analyzing clinical texts, enabling improved data extraction and understanding.

Considerations

1. **Data Privacy and Security**:
    - Ensure compliance with regulations like HIPAA to protect patient data and maintain confidentiality.
2. **Bias and Fairness**:
    - Address potential biases in training data that can lead to disparities in healthcare outcomes. Implement fairness-aware algorithms.
3. **Interpretability**:
    - Use interpretable models or explainability techniques to ensure that healthcare providers understand and trust ML predictions.
4. **Integration with Clinical Workflows**:
    - Ensure that ML solutions integrate smoothly with existing clinical systems and workflows to enhance usability and acceptance.
5. **Validation and Regulation**:
    - Rigorously validate ML models using clinical trials and adhere to medical device and software regulatory guidelines.
6. **Collaboration with Healthcare Professionals**:
    - Engage with clinicians and researchers to ensure that ML applications address real-world healthcare challenges effectively.

Conclusion

Machine learning is poised to revolutionize medical science by enhancing diagnostics, personalizing treatment, and improving operational efficiencies. By leveraging advanced ML techniques and collaborating with healthcare professionals, the potential for improving patient outcomes and optimizing healthcare delivery is significant. Continuous research and development will be crucial for harnessing the full capabilities of ML in the medical field.

Conventional Clinical Methods in Guiding Management of Heart Failure Patients

Heart failure (HF) is a complex clinical syndrome that requires careful management and monitoring. Conventional methods include clinical assessments, imaging, and biomarker measurements, but integrating machine learning (ML) can enhance these approaches, leading to improved patient outcomes. Here's an overview of how ML can complement traditional methods in managing heart failure.

Conventional Clinical Methods

1. **Clinical Assessments**:
    - **History and Physical Examination**: Physicians evaluate symptoms (e.g., dyspnea, fatigue), medical history, and perform physical exams to assess the severity of heart failure.
    - **Functional Classification**: The New York Heart Association (NYHA) classification helps determine the functional capacity of patients.
2. **Diagnostic Imaging**:
    - **Echocardiography**: Used to assess cardiac function, ejection fraction, and structural abnormalities.
    - **Cardiac MRI**: Provides detailed images of the heart's structure and function.

3. **Biomarker Measurements**:
   - **Natriuretic Peptides (e.g., BNP, NT-proBNP)**: Elevated levels indicate the severity of heart failure and can guide treatment decisions.
   - **Other Biomarkers**: Troponins, renal function markers, and electrolytes are monitored to assess patient status.
4. **Medication Management**:
   - **Guideline-Directed Medical Therapy (GDMT)**: Physicians prescribe medications like ACE inhibitors, beta-blockers, and diuretics based on clinical guidelines and individual patient factors.
5. **Lifestyle Modifications**:
   - Recommendations for dietary changes, exercise, and fluid management are integral to managing heart failure.

Integrating Machine Learning

Machine learning can enhance conventional methods by analyzing vast amounts of patient data to identify patterns, predict outcomes, and personalize treatment plans. Here are key applications:

1. **Risk Stratification**:
   - ML algorithms can analyze clinical, demographic, and biomarker data to identify patients at high risk for adverse outcomes, such as hospitalization or mortality.
2. **Predictive Modeling**:
   - Models can predict patient responses to treatments, enabling personalized medication management. For instance, predicting which patients are likely to benefit from specific heart failure medications.
3. **Continuous Monitoring**:
   - Wearable devices can collect real-time data (e.g., heart rate, activity level). ML algorithms can analyze this data to detect early signs of decompensation or worsening heart failure.
4. **Imaging Analysis**:
   - ML techniques, such as deep learning, can enhance the interpretation of echocardiograms and cardiac MRIs, improving the detection of structural abnormalities and functional impairment.

5. **Clinical Decision Support**:
   - Integrating ML with electronic health records (EHR) can provide clinicians with decision-support tools, offering evidence-based recommendations tailored to individual patient profiles.
6. **Symptom Prediction**:
   - ML can analyze historical symptom data to predict symptom exacerbation, allowing for timely interventions.

Benefits of Machine Learning in Heart Failure Management

- **Enhanced Accuracy**: ML models can identify subtle patterns in data that may be missed by conventional methods.
- **Personalization**: Tailoring treatment plans to individual patient characteristics can improve adherence and outcomes.
- **Early Intervention**: Predictive analytics can help identify patients at risk for worsening heart failure earlier, allowing for timely interventions.
- **Resource Optimization**: Improved risk stratification helps allocate healthcare resources more effectively, reducing unnecessary hospitalizations.

Challenges and Considerations

- **Data Quality and Availability**: High-quality, comprehensive datasets are essential for training accurate ML models.
- **Interpretability**: Many ML models are complex and may lack transparency, making it challenging for clinicians to understand the rationale behind predictions.
- **Integration into Clinical Workflow**: Seamless integration of ML tools into existing clinical workflows is necessary for widespread adoption.
- **Regulatory Considerations**: Ensuring compliance with regulations and guidelines when implementing ML solutions in clinical practice is crucial.

Conclusion

Integrating machine learning into conventional clinical methods for managing heart failure can significantly enhance patient care. By leveraging data-driven insights, healthcare providers can improve risk stratification, personalize treatments, and enable early interventions. As technology continues to evolve, the collaboration between clinicians and data scientists will be essential in developing and implementing effective ML solutions in heart failure management.

Neuroimaging to Improve Brain Health

Neuroimaging techniques, such as MRI, PET, and CT scans, are crucial for understanding brain health and diagnosing neurological conditions. Machine learning (ML) can enhance the analysis of neuroimaging data, leading to better insights into brain health, early disease detection, and personalized treatment strategies. Here's an overview of how ML can be applied in this field.

Key Neuroimaging Techniques

1. **Magnetic Resonance Imaging (MRI)**:
   - Provides detailed images of brain structures and can assess changes in brain volume and integrity.
   - Functional MRI (fMRI) measures brain activity by detecting changes in blood flow.
2. **Positron Emission Tomography (PET)**:
   - Measures metabolic processes in the brain, often used to detect Alzheimer's disease and other neurodegenerative disorders.
3. **Computed Tomography (CT)**:
   - Useful for quick assessment of brain injuries and hemorrhages, providing structural images of the brain.

Applications of Machine Learning in Neuroimaging

1. **Disease Diagnosis and Classification**:
    - ML algorithms can analyze neuroimaging data to classify brain diseases, such as Alzheimer's, Parkinson's, and multiple sclerosis, with high accuracy.
    - Deep learning models, particularly convolutional neural networks (CNNs), have shown promise in image classification tasks.
2. **Predicting Disease Progression**:
    - ML can identify patterns in neuroimaging data that correlate with disease progression, enabling predictions about the future course of neurological conditions.
3. **Brain Health Monitoring**:
    - Continuous monitoring using ML can track changes in brain structure and function over time, providing insights into the effectiveness of interventions and therapies.
4. **Identifying Biomarkers**:
    - ML techniques can uncover novel biomarkers for neurological diseases by analyzing neuroimaging data alongside genetic and clinical information.
5. **Personalized Treatment Plans**:
    - By integrating neuroimaging data with clinical and demographic information, ML can help develop personalized treatment plans tailored to individual patient profiles.
6. **Enhancing Imaging Techniques**:
    - ML algorithms can improve image quality, reduce noise, and enhance the resolution of neuroimaging scans, leading to more accurate diagnoses.

Techniques Used

1. **Supervised Learning**:
    - Used for classification tasks, such as differentiating between healthy and diseased brains based on neuroimaging features.
2. **Unsupervised Learning**:
    - Clustering algorithms can identify subtypes of neurological diseases based on imaging characteristics, facilitating more targeted research and treatment.

1. **Deep Learning**:
    - CNNs are particularly effective in analyzing image data and extracting complex features from neuroimaging scans to improve diagnostic accuracy.
2. **Reinforcement Learning**:
    - Can be applied in adaptive imaging protocols, optimizing scanning parameters based on real-time feedback.

Benefits of Machine Learning in Neuroimaging

- **Improved Diagnostic Accuracy**: ML can enhance the precision of diagnoses by identifying subtle patterns in neuroimaging data that may not be apparent to human observers.
- **Early Detection**: Identifying early signs of neurological conditions can lead to timely interventions, improving patient outcomes.
- **Increased Efficiency**: Automation of image analysis can reduce the workload for radiologists and speed up the diagnostic process.
- **Enhanced Research**: ML can facilitate large-scale studies by analyzing vast amounts of neuroimaging data, contributing to a deeper understanding of brain health.

Challenges and Considerations

- **Data Quality**: High-quality, annotated datasets are crucial for training effective ML models. Variability in imaging protocols and patient populations can affect model performance.
- **Interpretability**: Many ML models, especially deep learning ones, can be viewed as "black boxes," making it difficult to interpret their predictions in a clinical context.
- **Integration into Clinical Practice**: Seamless integration of ML tools into existing workflows is essential for their adoption by healthcare professionals.
- **Ethical Considerations**: Ensuring patient privacy and data security is critical, especially when handling sensitive neuroimaging data.

Conclusion

Machine learning has the potential to revolutionize the field of neuroimaging, leading to improved diagnosis, monitoring, and treatment of neurological conditions. By leveraging advanced algorithms to analyze complex imaging data, healthcare providers can enhance brain health outcomes and deliver more personalized care. Ongoing collaboration between neuroimaging experts, clinicians, and data scientists will be key to unlocking the full potential of ML in this domain.

Inferring Primary Care Relationships

Primary care relationships are fundamental to patient health outcomes, as they provide continuous, comprehensive care and coordination across different healthcare services. Machine learning (ML) can help infer these relationships by analyzing various data sources, enabling healthcare providers to understand patient interactions better and improve care delivery.

Key Objectives

1. **Identifying Patient-Provider Relationships**
   - Determine which patients are associated with specific primary care providers (PCPs) based on healthcare utilization patterns.
2. **Assessing Relationship Strength**
   - Evaluate the strength of the patient-PCP relationship by analyzing visit frequency, continuity of care, and patient engagement metrics.
3. **Predicting Patient Outcomes**
   - Use ML models to predict health outcomes based on the nature of the primary care relationship, such as hospitalization rates or management of chronic diseases.

Data Sources

1. **Electronic Health Records (EHRs)**
   - Data on patient visits, provider assignments, diagnoses, treatment plans, and follow-up activities.
2. **Claims Data**
   - Information on insurance claims can provide insights into healthcare utilization patterns and provider interactions.
3. **Patient Surveys**
   - Data from surveys can reveal patient satisfaction, engagement, and perceived quality of care.
4. **Demographic Data**
   - Information such as age, gender, socioeconomic status, and health history can help analyze relationships and predict outcomes.

Machine Learning Techniques

1. **Supervised Learning**
   - **Classification Algorithms:**
     - Logistic regression, decision trees, and random forests can classify patients based on their likelihood of having a strong relationship with their PCP.
   - **Regression Analysis:**
     - Models like linear regression can predict continuous outcomes, such as health status based on care relationship metrics.
2. **Unsupervised Learning**
   - **Clustering:**
     - K-means or hierarchical clustering can identify distinct groups of patients or providers based on care patterns, enabling the detection of relationship types or quality.
3. **Natural Language Processing (NLP)**
   - Analyze unstructured data from clinical notes to extract relevant information about patient-provider interactions and sentiments.
4. **Graph-Based Approaches**
   - Represent patients and providers as nodes in a graph, using graph algorithms to infer connections and relationships based on interaction data.

Applications

1. **Continuity of Care Analysis**
   - Use ML to analyze patterns of care continuity, identifying patients who may benefit from more consistent engagement with their PCP.
2. **Risk Stratification**
   - Predict patients at risk of poor outcomes based on the strength of their primary care relationships, allowing for targeted interventions.
3. **Improving Care Coordination**
   - Analyze patient pathways through the healthcare system to identify gaps or inefficiencies in care coordination.
4. **Patient Engagement Strategies**
   - Develop strategies for increasing patient engagement by understanding factors that strengthen relationships with PCPs.

Challenges and Considerations

1. **Data Privacy and Security**
   - Ensuring the confidentiality of patient data is paramount, especially when using EHRs and claims data.
2. **Data Quality**
   - The accuracy and completeness of data can significantly affect model performance. Data preprocessing and validation are essential.
3. **Model Interpretability**
   - Understanding and explaining ML model predictions in a clinical context is crucial for adoption by healthcare professionals.
4. **Integration into Clinical Practice**
   - Seamless integration of ML insights into existing workflows is necessary for practical applications in healthcare settings.

Conclusion

Machine learning offers valuable tools for inferring and analyzing primary care relationships, leading to improved patient outcomes and enhanced care coordination. By leveraging various data sources and advanced analytical techniques, healthcare providers can gain insights into patient interactions and optimize primary care delivery. Continued collaboration between data scientists and healthcare professionals will be essential to fully realize the potential of these innovations.

Prediction of Cardiovascular Death After Acute Coronary Syndrome

Acute coronary syndrome (ACS) encompasses a range of conditions associated with sudden, reduced blood flow to the heart, such as heart attacks. Predicting cardiovascular death following ACS is critical for improving patient outcomes and guiding treatment decisions. Machine learning (ML) techniques can enhance prediction accuracy by analyzing complex datasets and identifying patterns that traditional statistical methods may overlook.

Key Applications

1. **Risk Stratification**
   - **Patient Profiling:** ML algorithms can stratify patients based on their risk of cardiovascular death, enabling targeted interventions for high-risk individuals.
   - **Survival Analysis:** Models can predict survival rates based on clinical and demographic variables, improving prognostic accuracy.
2. **Early Warning Systems**
   - **Real-Time Monitoring:** ML can analyze continuous health data (e.g., vital signs, lab results) to provide real-time alerts for deteriorating conditions.
   - **Decision Support Systems:** Integrating ML predictions

into clinical workflows can assist healthcare providers in making timely decisions.

3. **Identifying Risk Factors**
    - **Feature Importance Analysis:** ML can highlight the most significant clinical and demographic factors contributing to cardiovascular mortality, guiding preventive strategies.
    - **Uncovering Hidden Patterns:** Advanced algorithms can discover complex interactions among risk factors that traditional analyses might miss.

Techniques Used

1. **Supervised Learning**
    - **Classification Algorithms:** Logistic regression, support vector machines, and random forests can classify patients as high or low risk for cardiovascular death based on historical data.
    - **Gradient Boosting Machines (GBM):** These models can enhance prediction accuracy by combining multiple weak learners into a robust predictor.
2. **Deep Learning**
    - **Neural Networks:** Deep learning models can analyze complex data patterns, such as imaging and genetic data, to improve predictions.
    - **Recurrent Neural Networks (RNNs):** Useful for sequential data, RNNs can track changes over time in patient health metrics.
3. **Survival Analysis Techniques**
    - **Cox Proportional Hazards Model:** While not strictly an ML technique, it can be combined with ML algorithms to analyze time-to-event data and assess risk factors.
    - **Random Survival Forests:** An extension of random forests for survival data, useful for predicting time until an event (e.g., cardiovascular death).

Data Sources

- **Clinical Data:** Patient demographics, medical history, laboratory results, and treatment information.

- **Imaging Data:** Cardiac MRI, CT scans, and echocardiograms can provide additional insights into heart function and structure.
- **Genomic Data:** Genetic information may reveal predispositions to cardiovascular diseases, enhancing risk assessment.

Challenges and Considerations

1. **Data Quality**
    - Ensuring high-quality, comprehensive datasets is critical for model training. Missing or inaccurate data can lead to biased predictions.
2. **Model Interpretability**
    - Many ML models, especially deep learning ones, can be complex and challenging to interpret. Techniques like SHAP and LIME can help provide insights into model predictions.
3. **Integration into Clinical Practice**
    - Incorporating ML predictions into existing clinical workflows requires careful planning and training for healthcare providers.
4. **Regulatory Compliance**
    - Adhering to healthcare regulations and standards is essential, particularly regarding patient data privacy and ethical considerations.
5. **Generalizability**
    - Models trained on specific populations may not generalize well to other patient groups, necessitating external validation.

Conclusion

Machine learning holds significant promise for predicting cardiovascular death after acute coronary syndrome, offering enhanced risk stratification, early warning systems, and insights into risk factors. By leveraging diverse data sources and advanced algorithms, healthcare providers can improve patient outcomes and guide effective interventions. Collaboration between data scientists, clinicians, and researchers will be vital for overcoming challenges and maximizing the potential of ML in cardiovascular medicine.

Continuously Monitored Physiological Data

The continuous monitoring of physiological data through wearable devices and sensors has transformed healthcare and personal wellness. Machine learning (ML) techniques can analyze this data to provide insights, detect anomalies, and even predict health events. Here's an overview of how ML can be applied to continuously monitored physiological data.

Key Physiological Data Types

1. **Heart Rate Variability (HRV):**
   - Measures the variation in time between heartbeats, reflecting autonomic nervous system activity.
2. **Blood Pressure:**
   - Continuous monitoring of systolic and diastolic pressure to assess cardiovascular health.
3. **Electrocardiogram (ECG):**
   - Measures electrical activity of the heart to detect arrhythmias and other heart conditions.
4. **Respiratory Rate:**
   - Monitors the number of breaths per minute, useful in assessing respiratory health.
5. **Body Temperature:**
   - Continuous temperature monitoring can indicate infections or other health issues.

6. **Activity Levels:**
    - Data from accelerometers and gyroscopes to track physical activity and sleep patterns.

Applications of Machine Learning

1. **Anomaly Detection:**
    - ML algorithms can identify deviations from normal physiological patterns, alerting healthcare providers or patients to potential health issues.
2. **Predictive Analytics:**
    - Using historical data to predict future health events, such as heart attacks or diabetic complications, enables proactive interventions.
3. **Health Monitoring:**
    - Continuous analysis of physiological data to track chronic conditions (e.g., hypertension, diabetes) and adjust treatment plans accordingly.
4. **Personalized Health Insights:**
    - Tailoring health recommendations based on individual physiological data, lifestyle, and preferences.
5. **Real-time Alerts:**
    - Sending notifications for critical changes in physiological parameters, enhancing patient safety.
6. **Behavioral Pattern Recognition:**
    - Analyzing data to identify lifestyle patterns and their impact on health, supporting preventive health measures.

Techniques Used

1. **Supervised Learning:**
    - Algorithms like logistic regression, decision trees, and neural networks can classify data (e.g., normal vs. abnormal heart rhythms).
2. **Unsupervised Learning:**
    - Clustering techniques can group similar physiological responses or identify patterns without labeled data.
3. **Time Series Analysis:**
    - Analyzing temporal data to detect trends, seasonality, and anomalies over time, especially in continuous data streams.

4. **Deep Learning:**
   - Recurrent Neural Networks (RNNs) and Long Short-Term Memory (LSTM) networks effectively predict sequence in time-series data, such as ECG signals.
5. **Ensemble Methods:**
   - Combining multiple models (e.g., Random Forest, Gradient Boosting) to improve accuracy and robustness.

Benefits of Using Machine Learning

- **Enhanced Accuracy:** ML models can analyze vast amounts of data, identifying subtle patterns that may be missed by human observers.
- **Early Detection:** Continuous monitoring allows for timely identification of health issues, improving outcomes through early intervention.
- **Efficiency:** Automating data analysis reduces the workload for healthcare professionals, allowing them to focus on patient care.
- **Personalization:** Tailored insights and recommendations can lead to better adherence to health regimens and improved patient engagement.

Challenges and Considerations

1. **Data Quality and Quantity:**
   - High-quality, labeled datasets are crucial for effective training of ML models. Incomplete or noisy data can lead to inaccurate predictions.
2. **Interpretability:**
   - Many ML models, particularly deep learning models, can be complex and hard to interpret. Ensuring transparency in decision-making is essential.
3. **Privacy and Security:**
   - Handling sensitive physiological data raises concerns about patient privacy and data security. Compliance with regulations (e.g., HIPAA) is critical.
4. **Integration into Healthcare Systems:**
   - Seamless integration of ML tools into existing healthcare workflows is necessary for practical application and adoption by clinicians.

5. **Ethical Considerations:**
   - Address potential biases in data and algorithms to ensure fair treatment across diverse patient populations.

Conclusion

Machine learning has the potential to revolutionize continuous physiological monitoring, enhance patient care, and enable proactive health management. By leveraging advanced algorithms to analyze real-time data, healthcare providers can deliver personalized insights, improve diagnostic accuracy, and foster better health outcomes. Ongoing collaboration between data scientists, healthcare professionals, and ethicists will be essential to navigating the challenges and unlocking the full potential of ML in this domain.

Patient Selection for Cardiac Resynchronization Therapy

Cardiac Resynchronization Therapy (CRT) is an effective treatment for patients with heart failure and left ventricular (LV) dyssynchrony. Selecting the right candidates for CRT can significantly improve patient outcomes. Machine learning (ML) can enhance the selection process by analyzing complex patient data to identify those most likely to benefit from the therapy.

Key Concepts

1. **Patient Characteristics:**
   - CRT is typically indicated for patients with:
     - Heart failure (NYHA Class II-IV)
     - Reduced ejection fraction (EF $\leq$ 35%)
     - QRS duration $\geq$ 130 ms (indicating electrical dyssynchrony)
2. **Data Sources:**
   - Patient demographics, clinical history, echocardiographic measurements, electrocardiograms (ECGs), and comorbidities.

Applications of Machine Learning

1. **Data Preprocessing:**
    - Clean and preprocess data, handling missing values and normalizing features. Feature selection is critical to identify relevant predictors of CRT response.
2. **Predictive Modeling:**
    - **Classification Algorithms:**
        - Use algorithms such as logistic regression, decision trees, random forests, and support vector machines (SVM) to classify patients as suitable or unsuitable candidates for CRT based on their clinical profiles.
    - **Ensemble Methods:**
        - Techniques like gradient boosting can improve predictive accuracy by combining multiple models.
3. **Risk Stratification:**
    - ML models can stratify patients based on their likelihood of responding to CRT, allowing for more tailored treatment plans.
4. **Outcome Prediction:**
    - Predict long-term outcomes (e.g., survival rates, quality of life improvements) for patients post-CRT, helping in the decision-making process.

Techniques Used

1. **Supervised Learning:**
    - **Logistic Regression:**
        - A baseline model for binary classification of CRT suitability.
    - **Random Forests:**
        - Effective for handling high-dimensional data and providing insights into feature importance.
    - **Gradient Boosting:**
        - Boosted trees can model complex interactions between features.
2. **Deep Learning:**
    - **Neural Networks:**
        - Can capture intricate patterns in large datasets, particularly

useful in analyzing imaging data or multivariate clinical features.

3. **Reinforcement Learning:**
   - Exploring adaptive treatment strategies based on ongoing patient data and responses.

Benefits of Machine Learning for CRT Patient Selection

- **Improved Prediction Accuracy:** ML models can identify subtle patterns in patient data that traditional criteria might miss, leading to better candidate selection.
- **Personalized Treatment Approaches:** Tailoring CRT decisions based on individual patient profiles can optimize treatment effectiveness.
- **Enhanced Decision Support:** Providing clinicians with data-driven insights can aid in the complex decision-making process regarding CRT candidacy.

Challenges and Considerations

1. **Data Quality and Quantity:**
   - High-quality, well-annotated datasets are essential for training effective ML models. Limited or biased datasets can lead to inaccurate predictions.
2. **Model Interpretability:**
   - It's crucial for healthcare providers to understand how ML models arrive at their recommendations. Techniques like SHAP or LIME can help elucidate model decisions.
3. **Integration into Clinical Practice:**
   - Seamless integration of ML tools into existing workflows and decision-making processes is necessary for adoption.
4. **Ethical Considerations:**
   - Addressing potential biases in training data is critical to ensure fair treatment recommendations across diverse patient populations.

Conclusion

Machine learning has the potential to significantly enhance patient selection for cardiac resynchronization therapy (CRT), leading to better outcomes for individuals with heart failure. By leveraging advanced algorithms to analyze complex clinical data, healthcare providers can make more informed decisions about CRT candidacy. Continued collaboration between data scientists and cardiologists will be essential in refining these models and ensuring their successful implementation in clinical settings.

Gesture Recognition Toolkit

Gesture recognition is a technology that interprets human gestures through mathematical algorithms, typically using sensors and machine learning techniques. A gesture recognition toolkit can be designed to facilitate the development of applications that require gesture input, such as in virtual reality, gaming, robotics, and human-computer interaction.

Key Components of a Gesture Recognition Toolkit

1. **Data Acquisition**:
   - **Sensors**: Use of cameras (RGB, depth), accelerometers, gyroscopes, and other motion sensors to capture gestures.
   - **Data Collection**: Tools to collect and preprocess gesture data, including recordings of various gestures performed by users.
2. **Preprocessing**:
   - **Normalization**: Scaling and transforming data to a standard format.
   - **Segmentation**: Dividing continuous gesture data into segments corresponding to individual gestures.
   - **Noise Reduction**: Applying filters to reduce noise in sensor data.

1. **Feature Extraction**:
    - **Key Points**: Identifying and extracting key points (e.g., fingertips, joints) from the data.
    - **Temporal Features**: Capturing the time series aspect of gestures, such as speed and acceleration.
    - **Statistical Features**: Calculating statistical properties (mean, variance) from gesture data.
2. **Machine Learning Models**:
    - **Classification Algorithms**:
        - **Supervised Learning**: Algorithms such as Support Vector Machines (SVM), Random Forests, and Neural Networks for classifying gestures based on labeled data.
        - **Deep Learning**: Convolutional Neural Networks (CNNs) or Recurrent Neural Networks (RNNs) for more complex gesture recognition tasks.
    - **Unsupervised Learning**: Clustering techniques for discovering gesture patterns without labeled data.
3. **Model Training and Validation**:
    - **Training**: Using labeled gesture data to train machine learning models.
    - **Validation**: Techniques like cross-validation to assess model performance and avoid overfitting.
4. **Integration and Deployment**:
    - **API Development**: Creating Application Programming Interfaces (APIs) for easy integration of gesture recognition into applications.
    - **Real-time Processing**: Ensuring models can process input data in real-time for responsive user experiences.
5. **User Interface**:
    - **Visualization Tools**: Interfaces for visualizing gesture data, model predictions, and performance metrics.
    - **Customization Options**: Allowing users to define and train custom gestures.

Frameworks and Libraries

- **OpenPose**: A library for real-time multi-person keypoint detection, useful for capturing human poses and gestures.
- **MediaPipe**: A framework by Google for building multimodal applied machine learning pipelines, including gesture recognition.

- **TensorFlow/Keras**: For building and training neural network models, with pre-built architectures for gesture classification.
- **PyTorch**: An alternative deep learning framework with strong support for dynamic computation graphs.
- **Scikit-learn**: Useful for traditional machine learning algorithms and preprocessing tasks.

Applications

1. **Virtual and Augmented Reality**: Enhancing user interaction through gesture controls.
2. **Smart Home Devices**: Enabling gesture-based control for appliances and systems.
3. **Gaming**: Allowing players to interact with games using natural gestures.
4. **Healthcare**: Assisting in rehabilitation through gesture recognition for physical therapy.
5. **Human-Robot Interaction**: Facilitating communication and control in robotics.

Challenges

- **Variability in Gestures**: Differences in how individuals perform gestures can impact recognition accuracy.
- **Environmental Factors**: Lighting, occlusion, and sensor noise can affect data quality.
- **Real-time Processing**: Achieving low latency for seamless user experience in applications.

Conclusion

A gesture recognition toolkit utilizing machine learning can significantly enhance user interactions across various domains. By integrating data acquisition, preprocessing, machine learning models, and user interfaces, developers can create robust applications that respond to human gestures intuitively and effectively. Ongoing research and advancements in machine learning and sensor technologies will continue to improve gesture recognition capabilities.

Biological Networks Using Machine Learning

Biological networks are complex systems of interactions between biological entities, such as genes, proteins, and metabolites. Understanding these networks is crucial for insights into cellular functions, disease mechanisms, and potential therapeutic targets. Machine learning (ML) offers powerful tools for analyzing and interpreting biological networks, enabling researchers to uncover patterns, predict interactions, and simulate biological processes. Here's an overview of how ML is applied in the context of biological networks.

1. Types of Biological Networks

- **Gene Regulatory Networks**: These networks illustrate how genes interact with each other and with regulatory elements to control gene expression.
- **Protein-Protein Interaction Networks**: These depict the physical interactions between proteins within a cell, crucial for understanding cellular processes.
- **Metabolic Networks**: These represent biochemical reactions and pathways within an organism, highlighting how metabolites are produced and consumed.
- **Pathway Networks**: These illustrate sequences of biochemical reactions and interactions that lead to specific biological outcomes, such as signal transduction or metabolic regulation.

2. Applications of Machine Learning in Biological Networks

- **Network Inference**: ML algorithms can be employed to predict interactions within biological networks from high-throughput data (e.g., transcriptomic or proteomic data). Techniques include:
  - **Graph-based models**: Such as Markov random fields and Bayesian networks.
  - **Deep learning**: Using neural networks to identify complex patterns in data.
- **Feature Selection**: Machine learning can help identify key features or nodes in a biological network that are most predictive of a particular outcome, such as disease susceptibility or drug response.
- **Pathway Enrichment Analysis**: ML can analyze the significance of biological pathways in high-dimensional datasets, providing insights into the underlying biology of diseases.
- **Predicting Biological Outcomes**: Supervised learning models can be trained to predict outcomes (e.g., drug efficacy or patient survival) based on the structure and dynamics of biological networks.
- **Simulation and Modeling**: Reinforcement learning and other ML techniques can be used to model dynamic biological processes, such as cellular responses to environmental changes or treatment regimens.

3. Machine Learning Techniques Used

- **Supervised Learning**: Techniques like decision trees, random forests, and support vector machines are used for classification and regression tasks based on labeled data.
- **Unsupervised Learning**: Clustering algorithms (e.g., k-means, hierarchical clustering) help identify subgroups within biological data, revealing hidden structures in networks.
- **Deep Learning**: Neural networks, especially convolutional and recurrent networks, are employed for tasks such as image analysis in bioinformatics or sequence data analysis.
- **Graph Neural Networks (GNNs)**: These models are specifically designed for processing graph-structured data, making them ideal for biological networks where relationships between entities are crucial.

4. Challenges and Considerations

- **Data Quality and Integration**: Biological data can be noisy and heterogeneous. Integrating data from multiple sources (e.g., genomics, proteomics, and clinical data) poses significant challenges.
- **Interpretability**: Many ML models, particularly deep learning ones, are often seen as "black boxes." Developing methods to interpret model outputs in a biological context is essential for gaining actionable insights.
- **Scalability**: As biological datasets grow larger, it is crucial to ensure that ML algorithms can scale appropriately while maintaining performance.
- **Biological Validation**: Predictions made by ML models must be experimentally validated to ensure their biological relevance and accuracy.

5. Future Directions

- **Integrative Approaches**: Combining ML with other computational techniques, such as systems biology or network pharmacology, to create comprehensive models of biological systems.
- **Real-time Analysis**: Leveraging ML for real-time analysis of biological data, especially in personalized medicine, where treatment decisions can be based on ongoing patient data.
- **Collaboration Across Disciplines**: Fostering collaboration between biologists, data scientists, and computational modelers to develop more robust biological network models.

Conclusion

Machine learning is transforming the analysis and understanding of biological networks, providing insights into complex biological processes and facilitating the development of new therapeutic strategies. As techniques advance and data continue to grow, the integration of ML in biological research will become increasingly essential, opening new avenues for discoveries in health and disease.

Drug Discovery Using Machine Learning

Drug discovery is a complex, multi-stage process that involves identifying new candidate medications. Traditionally, it relies heavily on experimental methods, which can be time-consuming and costly. Machine learning (ML) offers transformative capabilities that can accelerate this process by predicting molecular interactions, optimizing lead compounds, and more efficiently identifying potential drug candidates.

1. Key Stages of Drug Discovery

- **Target Identification**: Finding biological molecules (usually proteins) that are implicated in a disease.
- **Hit Identification**: Screening for compounds that interact with the target and exhibit desired biological activity.
- **Lead Optimization**: Refining hit compounds to improve their efficacy, safety, and pharmacokinetic properties.
- **Preclinical and Clinical Trials**: Testing compounds for safety and effectiveness in laboratory and clinical settings.

2. Applications of Machine Learning in Drug Discovery

A. Target Identification

- **Biological Data Mining**: ML algorithms can analyze large biological datasets (e.g., genomics, proteomics) to identify potential drug targets.
- **Gene Expression Analysis**: Using supervised learning to correlate gene expression patterns with disease states, highlighting potential therapeutic targets.

B. Hit Identification

- **Virtual Screening**: ML models can predict how small molecules interact with target proteins, reducing the need for extensive experimental screening.
    - **Quantitative Structure-Activity Relationship (QSAR)** models can correlate chemical structure with biological activity.
- **Compound Generation**: Generative models (e.g., GANs) can create novel molecular structures that may exhibit desired properties.

C. Lead Optimization

- **Property Prediction**: ML can predict key properties (e.g., solubility, toxicity, bioavailability) of lead compounds using regression techniques.
- **Simulations**: ML techniques can simulate molecular dynamics to study interactions between drug candidates and targets, allowing for better optimization.

D. Preclinical and Clinical Trials

- **Patient Stratification**: ML algorithms can analyze clinical data to identify which patient populations are most likely to respond to a given therapy.
- **Adverse Event Prediction**: Predicting potential side effects and adverse reactions using historical clinical data, enhancing safety assessments.

3. Techniques Used in ML for Drug Discovery

- **Supervised Learning**:
    - **Regression Models**: For predicting quantitative outcomes (e.g., IC50 values for potency).
    - **Classification Models**: For identifying active vs. inactive compounds based on biological activity.
- **Unsupervised Learning**:
    - **Clustering**: To group similar compounds or biological profiles, aiding in understanding structure-activity relationships.
- **Deep Learning**:
    - **Convolutional Neural Networks (CNNs)**: Effective for analyzing chemical structures and images of compounds.
    - **Recurrent Neural Networks (RNNs)**: Useful for sequential data, such as protein sequences or chemical synthesis pathways.
- **Reinforcement Learning**:
    - **Optimizing Drug Development**: Reinforcement learning can adaptively explore compound spaces to identify optimal lead candidates and guide synthetic pathways.

4. Challenges and Considerations

- **Data Quality**: High-quality, annotated datasets are essential for effective model training. Data variability can significantly impact model performance.
- **Interpretability**: Many ML models, particularly deep learning approaches, are often seen as "black boxes." Interpretability methods (like SHAP or LIME) are critical for building trust with researchers.
- **Integration with Existing Workflows**: ML tools need to seamlessly integrate into traditional drug discovery workflows for widespread adoption.
- **Regulatory Approval**: Models must meet regulatory standards for validation and robustness before they can be applied in clinical settings.

Conclusion

Machine learning is poised to revolutionize drug discovery by enhancing efficiency, accuracy, and cost-effectiveness. By leveraging vast biological datasets and advanced computational techniques, researchers can streamline the identification of potential drug candidates and optimize them for therapeutic use. Continued collaboration between data scientists and medicinal chemists will be essential to unlock the full potential of ML in drug discovery, ultimately leading to faster and more effective treatments for patients.

Trace Genetically Engineered DNA

The use of machine learning (ML) in tracing genetically engineered DNA (GED) has significant implications for biotechnology, agriculture, and regulatory compliance. By analyzing genetic sequences and patterns, ML can assist in identifying, predicting, and monitoring genetically modified organisms (GMOs) in various environments.

Key Applications

1. **Identification of Genetic Modifications**
   - **Sequence Analysis**: ML algorithms can analyze DNA sequences to identify specific genetic modifications. This involves training models on known GMO sequences to recognize engineered traits.
   - **Pattern Recognition**: Using techniques like convolutional neural networks (CNNs) to detect unique patterns in genomic data associated with genetic engineering.
2. **Monitoring GMO Spread**
   - **Environmental Surveillance**: ML can analyze samples from various environments (e.g., soil, water) to detect the presence and spread of GMOs.
   - **Predictive Modeling**: Models can predict how GMOs might spread in different ecosystems based on environmental variables and genetic data.

3. **Risk Assessment**
   - **Ecological Impact Analysis**: ML can assess the potential ecological impacts of GMOs by analyzing interaction patterns with native species.
   - **Traceability**: Ensuring that GMO products can be traced back to their source through supply chain analysis, helping in compliance with regulations.
4. **Data Integration and Analysis**
   - **Multi-Omics Integration**: Combining genomics, transcriptomics, and proteomics data using ML to provide a holistic view of the effects of genetic modifications.
   - **Big Data Analytics**: Handling large datasets from various genomic studies to derive actionable insights about GMOs.

Techniques Used

1. **Supervised Learning**
   - Algorithms like random forests, support vector machines (SVMs), and neural networks are trained on labeled datasets (e.g., known GMO and non-GMO sequences) to classify new data.
2. **Unsupervised Learning**
   - Clustering techniques (e.g., K-means, hierarchical clustering) can identify groups of similar genetic modifications, helping to characterize unknown GMOs.
3. **Deep Learning**
   - Deep learning models, particularly CNNs, can automatically learn features from genomic sequences, enabling more accurate predictions and classifications.
4. **Natural Language Processing (NLP)**
   - NLP techniques can analyze scientific literature and reports related to GMOs, extracting relevant data and trends for better understanding and traceability.

Benefits

- **Enhanced Accuracy**: ML models can identify subtle genetic modifications with high precision, improving the reliability of tracing efforts.

- **Scalability**: Machine learning approaches can quickly process large volumes of genomic data, making them suitable for large-scale agricultural applications.
- **Timeliness**: Rapid analysis of DNA sequences allows for quicker responses to potential ecological threats posed by GMOs.

Challenges and Considerations

1. **Data Quality and Availability**
   - High-quality, annotated datasets are essential for training effective ML models. Limited access to comprehensive genomic databases can hinder progress.
2. **Interpretability**
   - Many ML models, especially deep learning algorithms, operate as "black boxes," making it difficult to interpret their predictions in a biological context.
3. **Ethical and Regulatory Issues**
   - The application of ML in tracing GMOs raises ethical considerations regarding privacy, data security, and compliance with regulatory frameworks.
4. **Integration with Existing Systems**
   - Seamlessly integrating ML tools into current genetic monitoring and analysis workflows is crucial for adoption.

Conclusion

Machine learning offers powerful tools for tracing genetically engineered DNA, enabling better identification, monitoring, and risk assessment of GMOs. By leveraging advanced algorithms, researchers and regulators can enhance their understanding of genetic modifications and their impacts on ecosystems. However, addressing challenges related to data quality, interpretability, and ethical considerations is essential for successfully implementing these technologies. As the field evolves, collaboration among biologists, data scientists, and regulatory bodies will be crucial for optimizing the use of machine learning in this important area.

Retail order management Machine Learning

Machine learning (ML) can significantly enhance retail order management by improving inventory control, demand forecasting, and customer satisfaction. Here are some key applications, techniques, and considerations for using ML in this domain:

Key Applications

1. **Demand Forecasting**:
   - **Sales Predictions**: Use historical sales data to predict future demand for products, helping to optimize inventory levels.
   - **Seasonality and Trends**: Incorporate seasonal trends and promotional events into forecasting models.
2. **Inventory Management**:
   - **Stock Optimization**: Implement ML algorithms to maintain optimal stock levels, minimizing overstock and stockouts.
   - **Automated Reordering**: Predict when to reorder items based on demand forecasts and lead times.
3. **Order Processing**:
   - **Automated Order Fulfillment**: Use ML to streamline order fulfillment processes, optimize picking routes, and manage warehouses.
   - **Dynamic Pricing**: Adjust prices in real-time based on demand, inventory levels, and competitor pricing.

4. **Customer Segmentation**:
    - **Personalization**: Analyze customer behavior and preferences to tailor marketing strategies and product recommendations.
    - **Churn Prediction**: Identify at-risk customers using predictive analytics to implement retention strategies.
5. **Fraud Detection**:
    - **Transaction Monitoring**: Use anomaly detection to identify fraudulent transactions in order management systems.
6. **Supply Chain Optimization**:
    - **Supplier Performance**: Assess supplier reliability and optimize order quantities based on performance metrics.
    - **Logistics Optimization**: Use ML algorithms to enhance routing and delivery schedules, reducing costs and improving delivery times.

Techniques

1. **Supervised Learning**:
    - **Regression Models**: Predict sales or demand using historical data.
    - **Classification Algorithms**: Identify customer segments or predict order fulfillment success.
2. **Unsupervised Learning**:
    - **Clustering**: Group similar customers or products to enhance marketing and inventory strategies.
    - **Association Rule Learning**: Discover relationships between products (e.g., items frequently bought together).
3. **Time Series Analysis**:
    - **ARIMA Models**: Traditional time series forecasting methods to predict future demand based on historical trends.
    - **LSTM Networks**: Use deep learning for more complex time series forecasting tasks.
4. **Reinforcement Learning**:
    - Apply RL techniques for dynamic pricing and inventory management strategies that adapt based on real-time feedback.
5. **Natural Language Processing (NLP)**:
    - Analyze customer reviews and feedback to improve product offerings and customer service.

Considerations

1. **Data Quality**:
   - Ensure the data used for training models is accurate, complete, and relevant. Data preprocessing is crucial for effective ML applications.
2. **Integration with Existing Systems**:
   - ML solutions should be seamlessly integrated with existing order management and inventory systems for optimal performance.
3. **Scalability**:
   - Choose models and infrastructure that can scale with the growth of the business and increasing data volume.
4. **Model Interpretability**:
   - Utilize interpretable models or techniques (like SHAP or LIME) to explain predictions and recommendations to stakeholders.
5. **Regulatory Compliance**:
   - Adhere to data privacy regulations, especially when handling customer data for personalization and segmentation.
6. **Ethical Considerations**:
   - Ensure ML models do not propagate biases, particularly in customer segmentation and pricing strategies.

Conclusion

Machine learning can transform retail order management by improving forecasting accuracy, optimizing inventory, and enhancing customer experiences. By leveraging data effectively and implementing robust ML techniques, retailers can make informed decisions that drive efficiency and profitability. As the technology evolves, continuous evaluation and adaptation will be essential to keep pace with changing market conditions and customer expectations.

Demand Planning

Demand planning is a crucial aspect of supply chain management that involves forecasting customer demand to ensure the right amount of product is available at the right time. Machine learning (ML) has become an invaluable tool for enhancing demand planning processes. It provides more accurate forecasts and insights that can lead to improved inventory management, reduced costs, and increased customer satisfaction.

Key Concepts in Demand Planning

1. **Forecasting Demand:**
   - The process of predicting future customer demand based on historical sales data, market trends, and other influencing factors.
2. **Inventory Management:**
   - The supervision of non-capitalized assets, or inventory, and stock items to optimize the flow of goods.
3. **Supply Chain Optimization:**
   - Improving the efficiency of the supply chain by coordinating demand with supply, minimizing costs, and maximizing service levels.

Applications of Machine Learning in Demand Planning

1. **Sales Forecasting:**
    - ML algorithms can analyze historical sales data to identify patterns and trends, leading to more accurate sales forecasts.
    - Common models used include:
        - **Time Series Analysis:** Techniques like ARIMA or seasonal decomposition can be enhanced with ML for better accuracy.
        - **Regression Models:** Linear regression, support vector regression, and ensemble methods can predict future sales based on various factors.
2. **Demand Sensing:**
    - ML can provide near-real-time insights by analyzing data from various sources, including POS systems, social media, and weather forecasts, to adjust demand forecasts dynamically.
3. **Customer Segmentation:**
    - Businesses can tailor their demand planning strategies to different segments by clustering customers based on purchasing behavior and preferences.
4. **Promotion and Seasonality Impact:**
    - ML models can evaluate the effects of promotions, seasonality, and external factors (like economic indicators) on demand, improving forecasting during promotional periods.
5. **Inventory Optimization:**
    - ML can help determine optimal inventory levels by predicting future demand and identifying reorder points, thus reducing holding costs and stockouts.

Techniques Used

1. **Supervised Learning:**
    - Most demand forecasting models rely on historical data labeled with demand outcomes to train algorithms for predicting future demand.
2. **Unsupervised Learning:**
    - Clustering techniques can segment customers or products based on purchase patterns, aiding in demand planning strategies.

1. **Deep Learning:**
   - Neural networks, particularly recurrent neural networks (RNNs) and long short-term memory (LSTM) networks are effective for analyzing time series data and capturing complex patterns.
2. **Ensemble Methods:**
   - Techniques like random forests or gradient boosting can combine predictions from multiple models to improve accuracy and robustness.

Benefits of Using Machine Learning in Demand Planning

1. **Improved Accuracy:**
   - ML can significantly enhance forecasting accuracy by capturing nonlinear relationships and complex patterns in historical data.
2. **Adaptability:**
   - ML models can quickly adapt to changes in demand patterns, such as shifts in consumer preferences or market conditions, leading to more responsive planning.
3. **Data-Driven Insights:**
   - By analyzing a broader range of data sources (sales, social media, weather), ML provides richer insights that enhance decision-making.
4. **Cost Reduction:**
   - More accurate forecasts help minimize excess inventory and reduce the costs associated with stockouts or overstocking.

Challenges and Considerations

1. **Data Quality:**
   - The effectiveness of ML models relies heavily on the quality and completeness of the input data. Poor-quality data can lead to inaccurate forecasts.
2. **Model Complexity:**
   - More complex models may require more data and computational resources, potentially leading to overfitting if not managed carefully.

1. **Interpretability:**
    - Many ML models operate as "black boxes," making it difficult to understand how predictions are made. This can be a barrier to trust and adoption in business contexts.
2. **Integration with Existing Systems:**
    - Integrating ML solutions into existing demand planning and inventory management systems can be challenging and may require significant changes to workflows.

Conclusion

Machine learning is transforming demand planning by enabling organizations to forecast demand more accurately and respond quickly to market changes. By leveraging ML algorithms, businesses can improve inventory management, reduce costs, and enhance customer satisfaction. As technology advances, integrating ML into demand planning will become increasingly essential for organizations seeking to maintain a competitive edge in the market.

Forecasting Seasonal Footwear Demand

Accurate demand forecasting is essential for managing inventory and optimizing sales strategies in the footwear industry, particularly given the seasonal nature of fashion trends. Machine learning (ML) offers advanced techniques for analyzing historical sales data, identifying patterns, and predicting future demand. Here's a comprehensive guide to forecasting seasonal footwear demand using ML.

Key Steps in Implementing ML for Demand Forecasting

1. **Data Collection**
    - **Sales Data:** Historical sales figures segmented by product, size, color, and season.
    - **External Factors:** Weather data, economic indicators, and marketing campaign information.
    - **Customer Data:** Demographic information and purchasing behavior.
2. **Data Preprocessing**
    - **Cleaning the Data:** Handle missing values, correct inconsistencies, and remove duplicates.
    - **Feature Engineering:**
        - Create new features such as:
            - Lagged variables (previous sales figures).
            - Rolling averages (to smooth out seasonality).

            - Seasonal indicators (e.g., holidays, promotional events).
    - **Date Features:** Extract components like month, day of the week, and holidays to capture seasonal patterns.
3. **Exploratory Data Analysis (EDA)**
    - Visualize sales trends over time to identify seasonality and cyclical patterns.
    - Use correlation matrices to understand relationships between features.
    - Identify outliers that may affect model performance.
4. **Choosing Machine Learning Models**
    - Select appropriate ML algorithms based on the data characteristics:
        - **Time Series Forecasting Models:**
            - **ARIMA (Auto Regressive Integrated Moving Average):** Good for univariate time series data with trends and seasonality.
            - **SARIMA (Seasonal ARIMA):** Extends ARIMA to capture seasonal patterns.
        - **Machine Learning Models:**
            - **Random Forest:** Handles non-linear relationships and interactions effectively.
            - **Gradient Boosting Machines (e.g., XGBoost):** Powerful for structured data and capturing complex patterns.
            - **LSTM (Long Short-Term Memory) Networks:** Effective for sequential data and time series forecasting.
            - **Prophet:** Developed by Facebook for forecasting time series data with seasonality.
5. **Model Training and Validation**
    - Split the dataset into training and test sets, ensuring that the test set represents the most recent time period.
    - Train the selected models on the training set.
    - Validate performance using metrics such as:
        - **Mean Absolute Error (MAE):** Measures average magnitude of errors.
        - **Root Mean Squared Error (RMSE):** Penalizes larger errors more heavily.
        - **Mean Absolute Percentage Error (MAPE):** Provides a percentage-based error measurement.

1. **Hyperparameter Tuning**
   - Use techniques like Grid Search or Random Search to optimize model parameters for better performance.
2. **Making Predictions**
   - Use the trained model to forecast future footwear demand for the upcoming seasons.
   - Generate predictions at different granularities (daily, weekly, monthly) as needed.
3. **Visualization and Reporting**
   - Visualize forecasted demand alongside historical data to assess accuracy and trends.
   - Create dashboards to communicate insights to stakeholders, enabling data-driven decision-making.
4. **Integration and Continuous Improvement**
   - Integrate forecasts into inventory management and supply chain processes.
   - Monitor forecast accuracy and refine models regularly based on new data and changing market conditions.

Applications of Forecasting Seasonal Footwear Demand

1. **Inventory Management:**
   - Optimize stock levels to prevent overstocking or stockouts, especially during peak seasons.
2. **Supply Chain Optimization:**
   - Plan production schedules and logistics based on accurate demand forecasts.
3. **Marketing Strategies:**
   - Tailor marketing campaigns around predicted peaks in demand, enhancing promotional effectiveness.
4. **Product Development:**
   - Inform design and development of new styles based on anticipated trends and demand.
5. **Financial Planning:**
   - Support budget forecasting and financial decision-making by providing insights into expected sales.

Challenges and Considerations

- **Data Quality:** Ensure accurate, comprehensive datasets to improve model reliability.
- **Seasonal Variability:** Account for external factors, such as market trends, economic shifts, and changes in consumer behavior, that can impact demand.
- **Model Interpretability:** Use interpretable models or techniques to explain predictions to stakeholders.
- **Real-time Adaptation:** Incorporate mechanisms to adjust forecasts in real time as new data becomes available.

Conclusion

Machine learning offers powerful tools for forecasting seasonal footwear demand, enabling businesses to enhance their operational efficiency and strategic planning. By leveraging historical data and advanced algorithms, companies can better predict future trends, optimize inventory levels, and improve customer satisfaction. Continuous refinement of forecasting models based on new insights and market changes will be crucial for maintaining competitiveness in the dynamic footwear industry.

Predicting Shipping Time

Predicting shipping time is crucial for optimizing logistics, enhancing customer satisfaction, and improving supply chain efficiency. Machine learning (ML) can analyze vast amounts of historical shipping data to forecast delivery times accurately. Here's an overview of how ML can be applied in this context.

Key Concepts

1. **Shipping Time Factors:**
   - Various factors influence shipping time, including distance, mode of transportation, weather conditions, traffic, and warehouse processing times.
2. **Data Sources:**
   - Historical shipping records, GPS tracking data, customer orders, and real-time traffic and weather data can all be used to inform predictions.

Applications of Machine Learning

1. **Data Preprocessing:**
   - Clean and preprocess data to handle missing values, outliers, and categorical variables. Feature engineering may include

creating new features like average delivery times, distance calculations, and traffic conditions.

2. **Predictive Modeling:**
    - **Regression Analysis:**
        - Use algorithms such as linear regression, decision trees, or ensemble methods (like random forests and gradient boosting) to predict shipping times based on historical data.
    - **Time-Series Analysis:**
        - Employ time-series forecasting models (like ARIMA or LSTM networks) to account for trends and seasonality in shipping times.
3. **Real-Time Adjustments:**
    - Integrate real-time data (e.g., traffic updates, weather conditions) into the predictive models to adjust shipping time estimates dynamically.

Techniques Used

1. **Linear Regression:**
    - A simple yet effective method for predicting continuous variables, useful for establishing baseline predictions.
2. **Decision Trees:**
    - Can capture non-linear relationships between features and are interpretable, allowing for easy understanding of decision rules.
3. **Random Forests and Gradient Boosting:**
    - Ensemble methods that improve accuracy and robustness by combining multiple decision trees.
4. **Support Vector Regression (SVR):**
    - Effective for high-dimensional datasets, SVR can handle complex relationships between shipping factors and delivery times.
5. **Neural Networks:**
    - Deep learning models, such as feedforward neural networks, can learn complex patterns in large datasets, improving predictive power.
6. **LSTM Networks:**
    - Ideal for capturing temporal dependencies in time-series data, especially when predicting shipping times over extended periods.

Benefits of Machine Learning for Shipping Time Prediction

- **Improved Accuracy:** ML models can learn from historical data, providing more accurate shipping time predictions than traditional methods.
- **Enhanced Customer Satisfaction:** Accurate predictions can lead to better customer communication regarding expected delivery times.
- **Optimized Logistics:** Companies can better plan their resources and operations based on accurate shipping forecasts.
- **Dynamic Adjustments:** Real-time data integration allows for adaptive predictions, improving responsiveness to unforeseen delays.

Challenges and Considerations

1. **Data Quality:**
   - Ensuring high-quality, comprehensive datasets is critical. Poor data can lead to inaccurate predictions.
2. **Feature Selection:**
   - Identifying the right features to include in the model is essential for capturing the factors influencing shipping times.
3. **Model Interpretability:**
   - Stakeholders need to understand how predictions are made, especially in regulated industries. Using interpretable models or techniques like SHAP can help.
4. **Scalability:**
   - The solution should be scalable to handle increasing volumes of shipping data as the business grows.
5. **Integration with Existing Systems:**
   - Seamless integration with logistics management systems is necessary for effective implementation.

Conclusion

Machine learning offers a powerful approach to predicting shipping times, enabling businesses to enhance logistics operations and improve customer satisfaction. Organizations can develop accurate and adaptive predictive models by leveraging historical data and real-time information. Continued collaboration between data scientists and logistics professionals will be essential to address challenges and fully realize the potential of ML in shipping time prediction.

Approaches to Improve Long-Range Demand Forecasting

Long-range demand forecasting is essential for effective supply chain management, inventory control, and strategic planning. Machine learning (ML) techniques can significantly enhance the accuracy and reliability of long-range forecasts. Here are key approaches to improve long-range demand forecasting using ML:

1. Data Enrichment and Feature Engineering

- **Incorporate External Data**: Augment demand data with external factors such as economic indicators, weather conditions, and market trends. For example, using economic data can help predict changes in consumer behavior.
- **Create Time-Based Features**: Generate features based on time, such as day of the week, month, holidays, and seasonal patterns. This can help capture temporal effects in demand.
- **Lagged Variables**: Include lagged demand values to help capture trends and cyclical patterns over time.

2. Advanced Machine Learning Models

- **Ensemble Methods**: Utilize techniques like Random Forests and Gradient Boosting Machines (GBM) that combine multiple models to improve prediction accuracy.

- **Deep Learning**: Implement Recurrent Neural Networks (RNNs) or Long Short-Term Memory (LSTM) networks, which effectively capture temporal dependencies in sequential data.
- **Transformers**: Explore transformer-based architectures, which have shown promise in handling long sequences and can capture complex relationships in time series data.

3. Hybrid Forecasting Models

- **Combining Statistical and ML Approaches**: Use statistical methods like ARIMA to capture trends and seasonality, and then apply ML models to the residuals to improve forecasts.
- **Model Stacking**: Create a stacked model where predictions from various models (statistical and ML) are combined to enhance overall accuracy.

4. Scenario Analysis and Simulation

- **What-If Analysis**: Use ML models to run simulations based on different scenarios (e.g., market changes, promotional events) to understand potential impacts on demand.
- **Monte Carlo Simulations**: Implement simulations that incorporate uncertainty in input variables, providing a range of potential outcomes.

5. Reinforcement Learning

- **Adaptive Forecasting**: Use reinforcement learning algorithms that adaptively learn from changing demand patterns over time, continuously improving the forecasting model based on real-time data.

6. Cross-Validation and Hyperparameter Tuning

- **Robust Validation Techniques**: Implement cross-validation methods tailored for time series data, such as time-based cross-validation, to assess model performance.
- **Hyperparameter Optimization**: Use techniques like Grid Search or Bayesian Optimization to fine-tune model parameters for improved accuracy.

7. Long-Term Trends and Seasonality

- **Decomposition Techniques**: Use decomposition methods (e.g., STL decomposition) to separate the long-term trend, seasonal components, and residuals, allowing models to focus on each aspect.
- **Trend Analysis**: Implement models that explicitly capture long-term trends, such as polynomial regression or trend-adjusted exponential smoothing.

8. Continuous Learning and Adaptation

- **Real-Time Data Integration**: Continuously update models with new data to adapt to changing trends and patterns, ensuring forecasts remain relevant.
- **Feedback Loops**: Create mechanisms to assess forecast accuracy regularly and adjust models accordingly based on feedback.

9. Explainability and Interpretability

- **Model Interpretability Tools**: Utilize tools like SHAP (SHapley Additive exPlanations) or LIME (Local Interpretable Model-agnostic Explanations) to understand model predictions and ensure transparency in decision-making.

Conclusion

Improving long-range demand forecasting with machine learning involves combining advanced modeling techniques, data enrichment, and continuous adaptation. By leveraging these approaches, organizations can achieve more accurate forecasts, leading to better inventory management, reduced costs, and improved customer satisfaction. Continuous research and adaptation to new data and trends are vital for maintaining the effectiveness of demand forecasting strategies.

Radio Frequency Integrated Circuits (RFIC) Development Using Machine Learning

Radio Frequency Integrated Circuits (RFICs) are crucial components in modern communication systems, enabling wireless communication in devices such as smartphones, IoT devices, and radar systems. The development of RFICs involves complex design challenges, including circuit performance, power consumption, and integration with other components. Machine learning (ML) offers innovative techniques to streamline the RFIC design process, optimize performance, and reduce time-to-market.

1. Overview of RFIC Development

- **Key Components**: RFICs typically include amplifiers, mixers, oscillators, and filters, which operate at high frequencies.
- **Design Challenges**:
  - **Nonlinearity**: RF circuits often exhibit nonlinear behavior that complicates analysis and optimization.
  - **Integration**: RFICs must integrate seamlessly with digital and analog components, requiring careful consideration of layout and interconnects.
  - **Variability**: Manufacturing variations can significantly affect circuit performance, necessitating robust design practices.

2. Machine Learning Applications in RFIC Development

A. Design Optimization

- **Parameter Tuning**: ML algorithms can optimize circuit parameters (e.g., biasing, component values) to achieve desired performance metrics (gain, bandwidth, efficiency).
- **Surrogate Models**: Use ML models to approximate complex RF behaviors, allowing for faster simulations and design iterations.

B. Data-Driven Design

- **Feature Extraction**: Analyze historical design data to identify key features that influence RF performance, helping engineers make informed design choices.
- **Generative Design**: Employ ML techniques to generate new design concepts based on learned patterns from existing successful RFIC designs.

C. Performance Prediction

- **Regression Models**: Use supervised learning to predict performance metrics (e.g., gain, noise figure) based on design parameters, enabling quicker evaluation of design changes.
- **Classification Models**: Classify designs into categories based on performance thresholds, helping to filter out suboptimal designs early in the process.

D. Anomaly Detection

- **Quality Assurance**: Implement ML techniques to monitor manufacturing processes, detecting anomalies that could lead to defects in RFIC production.
- **Reliability Assessment**: Use ML to predict potential failure modes based on operational data, enhancing reliability and longevity of RFICs.

3. Techniques Used in ML for RFIC Development

- **Supervised Learning**:
  - **Regression**: For performance prediction and optimization tasks.
  - **Classification**: For categorizing designs based on performance metrics.
- **Unsupervised Learning**:
  - **Clustering**: To group similar designs, helping in understanding design space and variability.
- **Deep Learning**:
  - **Neural Networks**: Effective for complex pattern recognition in high-dimensional data, especially in predicting performance based on multiple design parameters.
- **Reinforcement Learning**:
  - **Adaptive Design Processes**: Use reinforcement learning to iteratively improve designs based on feedback from performance evaluations.

4. Implementation Steps

1. **Data Collection**: Gather historical design data, performance metrics, and manufacturing information from previous RFIC projects.
2. **Data Preprocessing**: Clean and preprocess data to ensure quality, focusing on relevant features that influence RF performance.
3. **Model Selection**: Choose appropriate ML models based on the specific application (e.g., regression for performance prediction, clustering for design classification).
4. **Training and Validation**: Train ML models on the dataset, validating their performance through cross-validation techniques.
5. **Integration**: Integrate ML models into the RFIC design workflow, providing engineers with tools to utilize insights and predictions.
6. **Continuous Improvement**: Regularly update models with new data from ongoing projects to enhance accuracy and adaptability.

5. Challenges and Considerations

- **Data Quality**: Ensuring high-quality and representative datasets is critical for effective model training.
- **Model Interpretability**: RF engineers need to understand and trust ML model predictions; techniques for model interpretability (e.g., SHAP values) can aid in this.
- **Integration with Existing Tools**: Seamless integration of ML tools into existing RFIC design software and workflows is essential for widespread adoption.
- **Validation Against Physical Prototypes**: It's crucial to validate ML predictions with physical prototypes to ensure reliability.

6. Conclusion

The application of machine learning in RFIC development has the potential to transform the design process, making it more efficient and responsive to market needs. By leveraging data-driven insights and advanced algorithms, engineers can optimize RF circuit performance, reduce time-to-market, and enhance product reliability. As ML technologies continue to evolve, their integration into RFIC design will play a key role in advancing communication technologies. Ongoing collaboration between RF engineers and data scientists will be essential to fully realizing these benefits.

Materials Science Using Supervised Machine Learning

Materials science is increasingly leveraging supervised machine learning (ML) techniques to accelerate the discovery, design, and optimization of materials. By utilizing data-driven approaches, researchers can uncover relationships between material properties, structures, and processing conditions, leading to innovations across various fields, including electronics, energy, and biomaterials.

Key Applications

1. **Property Prediction**
   - **Objective:** Predict physical, chemical, and mechanical properties of materials based on their composition and structure.
   - **Methods:** Regression algorithms (e.g., linear regression, support vector regression) and neural networks can model the relationship between material descriptors and properties.
   - **Examples:** Predicting tensile strength, thermal conductivity, or electronic band gap.
2. **Material Discovery**
   - **Objective:** Identify new materials with desired properties using historical data and databases.
   - **Methods:** Classification algorithms (e.g., decision trees,

random forests) can be used to classify materials based on performance metrics or suitability for specific applications.
- **Examples:** Discovering new alloys or polymers for specific applications like batteries or lightweight structures.

3. **Process Optimization**
   - **Objective:** Optimize manufacturing processes to achieve desired material properties.
   - **Methods:** Supervised learning can help model the effects of processing parameters on material outcomes.
   - **Examples:** Optimizing heat treatment processes or additive manufacturing parameters to enhance mechanical properties.
4. **Failure Prediction**
   - **Objective:** Predict failure modes and lifetimes of materials in service.
   - **Methods:** Supervised models can analyze historical failure data to identify conditions that lead to material degradation or failure.
   - **Examples:** Predicting fatigue life in metals or polymer degradation under environmental stress.
5. **Materials Characterization**
   - **Objective:** Automate and enhance the analysis of materials characterization data.
   - **Methods:** ML techniques can classify and analyze data from techniques like X-ray diffraction (XRD) or scanning electron microscopy (SEM).
   - **Examples:** Identifying crystal structures or grain sizes from image data.

Techniques and Algorithms

1. **Linear Regression**
   - Used for predicting continuous properties based on linear relationships between features.
2. **Support Vector Machines (SVM)**
   - Effective for classification tasks, especially in high-dimensional spaces.
3. **Random Forests**
   - Ensemble method that improves prediction accuracy and handles non-linear relationships well.

4. **Neural Networks**
   - Particularly useful for capturing complex, non-linear relationships in large datasets, applicable in both regression and classification tasks.
5. **k-Nearest Neighbors (k-NN)**
   - A simple yet effective method for classification and regression, particularly useful in cases with less data.

Data Sources

- **Databases:** Materials Project, AFLOW, and other repositories provide extensive datasets of material properties and structures.
- **Experimental Data:** Collecting data from laboratory experiments and simulations can supplement existing datasets.

Challenges and Considerations

1. **Data Quality and Quantity**
   - High-quality, labeled datasets are crucial for effective training. Data cleaning and preprocessing may be necessary.
2. **Interpretability**
   - Many ML models, especially deep learning, can be challenging to interpret. Techniques like SHAP or LIME can help understand model predictions.
3. **Overfitting**
   - Models may overfit to training data, especially with limited data. Regularization techniques and cross-validation are essential.
4. **Generalization**
   - Ensuring models can generalize to unseen materials or conditions is vital for practical applications.
5. **Collaboration**
   - Interdisciplinary collaboration between materials scientists and data scientists is essential to ensure that ML models are grounded in physical principles.

Conclusion

Supervised machine learning offers powerful tools for advancing materials science by enhancing the prediction and optimization of material properties and processes. As data availability and computational resources continue to grow, integrating ML into materials research will likely lead to significant breakthroughs in material design and application. Ongoing collaboration between experts in materials science and machine learning will be key to maximizing the potential of these technologies.

Predicting Material Properties and Interatomic Potentials

Machine learning (ML) has emerged as a powerful tool in materials science, particularly for predicting material properties and interatomic potentials. These applications are crucial for understanding and designing materials with desired characteristics, impacting various fields, including nanotechnology, metallurgy, and polymer science.

Key Concepts

1. **Interatomic Potentials:**
   - Mathematical functions that describe the interactions between atoms in a material. They are essential for simulating material behavior in computational materials science.
2. **Material Properties:**
   - Characteristics of materials, such as mechanical strength, thermal conductivity, and electrical properties, that are critical for their applications.

Applications of Machine Learning in Materials Science

1. **Predicting Interatomic Potentials:**
   - Traditional methods, like density functional theory (DFT), can be computationally expensive. ML models can approximate these potentials more efficiently.

- Common ML models used include:
  - **Gaussian Approximation Potentials (GAP):** A framework that uses Gaussian process regression to model interatomic potentials.
  - **Neural Network Potentials:** Neural networks can be trained on data generated from DFT calculations to predict atomic interactions.
  - **Message Passing Neural Networks (MPNN):** These networks consider the connectivity between atoms and can capture complex interactions.

2. **Property Prediction:**
   - ML models can be trained on existing material datasets to predict properties based on atomic structure and composition.
   - Techniques include:
     - **Regression Models:** Such as support vector regression and random forests, used to predict continuous properties like thermal conductivity or elastic modulus.
     - **Classification Models:** Used for predicting categorical properties, like whether a material is ductile or brittle.
3. **Accelerated Materials Discovery:**
   - ML can help in the discovery of new materials by predicting properties of hypothetical compounds, significantly speeding up the research process.
   - High-throughput screening methods can evaluate thousands of compounds rapidly using ML predictions.

Techniques Used

1. **Supervised Learning:**
   - Most common approach where labeled datasets of atomic configurations and their corresponding properties or potentials are used to train models.
2. **Unsupervised Learning:**
   - Techniques like clustering can identify patterns in material data, helping to understand the relationships between different material properties.
3. **Deep Learning:**
   - Neural networks, especially convolutional and recurrent networks, effectively capture complex relationships in high-dimensional data.

4. **Transfer Learning:**
    - Utilizing pre-trained models on similar tasks can improve the efficiency and accuracy of predictions for new materials.

Benefits of Using Machine Learning in Materials Science

1. **Increased Efficiency:**
    - ML models can perform predictions much faster than traditional computational methods, allowing for rapid exploration of material properties.
2. **Improved Accuracy:**
    - When trained on high-quality datasets, ML models can achieve high accuracy in predicting material behavior, often outperforming traditional methods.
3. **Scalability:**
    - ML methods can quickly scale to analyze large datasets generated from experiments or simulations.
4. **Insights into Complex Systems:**
    - ML can uncover hidden patterns and relationships in complex material systems that may not be readily apparent through traditional analysis.

Challenges and Considerations

1. **Data Quality and Availability:**
    - High-quality, well-annotated datasets are essential for training effective ML models. Data from simulations or experiments can be noisy or incomplete.
2. **Model Interpretability:**
    - Many ML models function as "black boxes," making it difficult to understand how they arrive at predictions. Efforts must be made to enhance interpretability.
3. **Generalization:**
    - Models trained on specific datasets may not generalize well to different material systems or configurations. Careful validation and testing are necessary.
4. **Computational Resources:**
    - While ML models can speed up predictions, training complex models requires significant computational resources, especially for large datasets.

Conclusion

Machine learning is transforming the field of materials science by providing advanced methods for predicting material properties and interatomic potentials. By leveraging ML, researchers can accelerate materials discovery, enhance simulations, and gain deeper insights into material behavior. As data availability and computational techniques continue to improve, the impact of ML on materials science is expected to grow, opening new avenues for innovation and discovery.

Predictive Maintenance of Wind Turbines

Predictive maintenance leverages machine learning (ML) to anticipate equipment failures before they occur, optimizing maintenance schedules and reducing downtime. In the context of wind turbines, effective predictive maintenance can significantly enhance operational efficiency, reduce costs, and improve energy production. Here's a detailed overview of how ML can be applied to predictive maintenance for wind turbines.

Key Challenges in Wind Turbine Maintenance

1. **Complexity of Systems:**
   - Wind turbines consist of various components (e.g., rotor, gearbox, generator) that can fail in different ways.
2. **Harsh Operating Conditions:**
   - Turbines are often located in remote areas and exposed to extreme weather, leading to wear and tear.
3. **High Maintenance Costs:**
   - Unplanned downtime and repairs can be expensive, impacting profitability.
4. **Data Volume:**
   - Wind turbines generate vast amounts of data from sensors and monitoring systems, requiring efficient analysis techniques.

Machine Learning Applications

1. **Anomaly Detection:**
    - ML algorithms can analyze sensor data to detect abnormal patterns indicating potential failures. Techniques such as clustering and outlier detection can identify anomalies in operational data.
2. **Failure Prediction:**
    - Supervised learning models (e.g., logistic regression, decision trees, random forests) can be trained on historical failure data to predict future failures based on sensor readings and environmental conditions.
3. **Remaining Useful Life (RUL) Estimation:**
    - Using regression models, ML can estimate the remaining useful life of turbine components, helping prioritize maintenance activities.
4. **Root Cause Analysis:**
    - ML algorithms can help identify the root causes of failures by analyzing correlations between different sensor readings and environmental factors.
5. **Optimization of Maintenance Schedules:**
    - Reinforcement learning can be used to optimize maintenance scheduling based on predicted failure probabilities, balancing maintenance costs with operational reliability.
6. **Performance Monitoring:**
    - Continuous monitoring of turbine performance using ML can help detect efficiency losses, prompting maintenance actions before major failures occur.

Techniques Used

1. **Supervised Learning:**
    - Models like random forests, support vector machines (SVM), and neural networks are trained on labeled datasets to classify failure types and predict future failures.
2. **Unsupervised Learning:**
    - Clustering techniques (e.g., K-means, hierarchical clustering) can group similar operational states and identify patterns in the absence of labeled data.

1. **Time Series Analysis:**
   - Analyzing time-series data from sensors (e.g., vibration, temperature, RPM) to detect trends, seasonal patterns, and anomalies.
2. **Deep Learning:**
   - Convolutional Neural Networks (CNNs) can be used for image data from visual inspections, while Recurrent Neural Networks (RNNs) and LSTMs are effective for sequential sensor data.
3. **Ensemble Methods:**
   - Combining multiple models to improve accuracy and robustness in predictions.

Benefits of Using Machine Learning for Predictive Maintenance

- **Reduced Downtime:** By anticipating failures, maintenance can be scheduled proactively, minimizing operational disruptions.
- **Cost Savings:** Efficient maintenance strategies can lower repair costs and extend the lifespan of turbine components.
- **Increased Reliability:** Continuous monitoring and timely interventions enhance the overall reliability of wind turbine operations.
- **Optimized Resource Allocation:** Maintenance resources can be allocated more effectively based on predictive insights.

Challenges and Considerations

1. **Data Quality:**
   - High-quality, well-labeled datasets are essential for training effective ML models. Issues with missing or noisy data can hinder performance.
2. **Interpretability:**
   - Many ML models can be complex and difficult to interpret. Ensuring that maintenance personnel understand model predictions is critical for effective decision-making.
3. **Integration with Existing Systems:**
   - Seamless integration of ML solutions into existing turbine monitoring and maintenance systems is necessary for practical application.

1. **Scalability:**
   - As more turbines are added to the fleet, ML models must scale effectively to handle increased data volumes and complexity.
2. **Ethical Considerations:**
   - Ensuring fairness and accountability in decision-making processes based on ML predictions is important, particularly in resource allocation.

Conclusion

Machine learning offers transformative potential for predictive maintenance in wind turbines. It enables operators to optimize performance, reduce costs, and enhance reliability. By leveraging data-driven insights, the wind energy sector can advance towards more efficient and sustainable operations. Ongoing collaboration between data scientists, engineers, and industry stakeholders will be crucial to addressing challenges and maximizing the benefits of ML in predictive maintenance.

Oceanic Eddy Detection and Lifetime Forecast

Oceanic eddies are swirling bodies of water that play a critical role in ocean dynamics, influencing climate, marine ecosystems, and weather patterns. Detecting these eddies and predicting their lifetimes can enhance our understanding of ocean behavior and improve climate models. Machine learning (ML) offers powerful tools for analyzing oceanic data, facilitating the detection and forecasting of eddies. Here's an overview of how ML can be applied in this context.

Key Concepts

1. **Eddy Detection:**
   - Eddies can be identified in oceanographic data through patterns in temperature, salinity, and currents. Accurate detection is essential for understanding their impact on marine environments.
2. **Lifetime Forecasting:**
   - Predicting the lifespan of eddies is crucial for understanding their influence on oceanic processes and for resource management in fisheries and shipping.

Applications of Machine Learning

1. **Data Processing and Feature Extraction:**
    - ML algorithms can process large datasets from satellite imagery, buoy data, and oceanographic models to extract relevant features for eddy detection.
2. **Eddy Detection Models:**
    - **Supervised Learning:**
        - Models such as convolutional neural networks (CNNs) can be trained on labeled datasets (e.g., historical eddy positions) to classify eddies from oceanographic data.
    - **Unsupervised Learning:**
        - Clustering techniques (e.g., K-means) can help identify eddy patterns without prior labeling, facilitating the detection of new or less understood eddy types.
3. **Lifetime Prediction Models:**
    - **Regression Analysis:**
        - Techniques such as linear regression, random forests, or support vector regression can be employed to predict the lifetime of detected eddies based on their initial characteristics (size, intensity, and environmental factors).
    - **Time-Series Forecasting:**
        - Recurrent Neural Networks (RNNs) or Long Short-Term Memory (LSTM) networks can analyze temporal data to forecast future states of eddies based on historical patterns.
4. **Integration of Multimodal Data:**
    - Combining data from various sources (e.g., satellite observations, buoys, and model simulations) can enhance the accuracy of detection and forecasting models.

Techniques Used

1. **Convolutional Neural Networks (CNNs):**
    - Effective for image data, CNNs can automatically learn spatial hierarchies of features, making them suitable for analyzing satellite images of ocean surface conditions.
2. **Random Forests and Gradient Boosting:**
    - Ensemble methods can handle non-linear relationships and interactions between features, improving predictive accuracy for lifetime forecasts.

3. **Clustering Algorithms:**
    - Used for identifying eddy patterns in large datasets without predefined labels, aiding in exploratory analysis.
4. **Support Vector Machines (SVM):**
    - Can classify eddies based on features derived from environmental conditions, helping to distinguish between different eddy types.
5. **LSTM Networks:**
    - Suitable for time-series analysis, LSTMs can capture long-term dependencies in sequential data, improving lifetime predictions.

Benefits of Machine Learning for Eddy Detection and Forecasting

- **Improved Detection Accuracy:** ML algorithms can analyze complex datasets and detect subtle patterns that traditional methods may overlook.
- **Faster Processing:** Automated ML methods can process large volumes of data more quickly than manual approaches, facilitating real-time applications.
- **Enhanced Predictive Capabilities:** ML models can learn from historical data to make more accurate lifetime forecasts, aiding in decision-making for marine operations.
- **Scalability:** Machine learning can be applied to datasets of varying sizes, making it adaptable to different oceanographic conditions and research needs.

Challenges and Considerations

1. **Data Quality and Availability:**
    - High-quality, well-annotated datasets are crucial for training effective ML models. Issues like missing or noisy data can impact performance.
2. **Interpretability:**
    - Many ML models, especially deep learning ones, can act as "black boxes." Ensuring interpretability is vital for gaining trust from oceanographers and stakeholders.

1. **Integration with Existing Systems:**
   - Implementing ML solutions into existing oceanographic research and monitoring frameworks requires careful planning and collaboration.
2. **Computational Resources:**
   - Training complex ML models, especially on large datasets, may require significant computational power and resources.
3. **Environmental Variability:**
   - Ocean conditions can vary significantly; models must be robust enough to generalize across different regions and times.

Conclusion

Machine learning presents a transformative opportunity for oceanic eddy detection and lifetime forecasting. By leveraging advanced algorithms to analyze complex oceanographic data, researchers can enhance their understanding of eddy dynamics, leading to improved climate models and better resource management. Collaboration between data scientists and oceanographers will be essential to address challenges and maximize the benefits of ML in this field.

Demographic Bias Detection and Analysis

Demographic bias is the systematic discrimination or unfair treatment of specific demographic groups by machine learning models. Understanding and mitigating this bias is essential for developing fair and equitable AI systems. Here's how machine learning can be used to detect, analyze, and address demographic bias.

Understanding Demographic Bias

Demographic bias can manifest in various forms, such as:

- **Representation Bias**: Underrepresentation of certain groups in training data.
- **Measurement Bias**: Inaccurate data collection methods that may favor certain demographics.
- **Algorithmic Bias**: Models that learn biased patterns from training data and make unfair predictions.

Detecting Demographic Bias

1. **Performance Metrics**:
   - Use metrics such as accuracy, precision, recall, and F1-score across different demographic groups to identify disparities in model performance.

- Calculate specific fairness metrics, including:
  - **Demographic Parity**: The proportion of positive predictions across demographic groups.
  - **Equal Opportunity**: The true positive rate for each demographic group.

2. **Disparate Impact Analysis**:
   - Analyze the impact of model predictions on different demographic groups using statistical tests (e.g., Chi-square tests) to assess whether the model's predictions lead to disproportionate outcomes.
3. **Fairness Audits**:
   - Conduct audits on existing models by evaluating their predictions on labeled datasets stratified by demographic characteristics.
4. **Visualizations**:
   - Use graphical representations (e.g., confusion matrices, ROC curves) to visually compare performance across demographic groups.

Analyzing Demographic Bias

1. **Feature Importance Analysis**:
   - Use algorithms (e.g., SHAP, LIME) to assess how demographic features influence predictions, identifying whether they contribute to biased outcomes.
2. **Adversarial Testing**:
   - Implement adversarial techniques where models are tested against altered inputs to see if changes in demographic features disproportionately affect predictions.
3. **Clustering Techniques**:
   - Apply clustering algorithms (e.g., K-means, hierarchical clustering) to identify patterns within demographic groups, exploring how they differ in terms of model predictions.

Mitigating Demographic Bias

1. **Preprocessing Techniques**:
   - **Reweighing**: Adjust the weights of training samples to ensure balanced representation of demographic groups.

  - **Data Augmentation**: Generate synthetic data to balance underrepresented groups.
2. **In-processing Techniques**:
   - **Fairness Constraints**: Integrate fairness constraints directly into the training process (e.g., Fair Support Vector Machines).
   - **Regularization**: Use regularization methods that penalize bias in the training process.
3. **Post-processing Techniques**:
   - Adjust model outputs to ensure fairness after training. This may involve equalizing odds or adjusting thresholds for different demographic groups.

Monitoring and Evaluation

- **Continuous Monitoring**: Regularly assess models post-deployment for demographic bias as new data comes in.
- **Feedback Mechanisms**: Incorporate feedback from affected groups to identify and address biases that may not be captured through quantitative measures.

Ethical Considerations

1. **Transparency**: Ensure that model decisions are interpretable and can be explained to stakeholders.
2. **Data Privacy**: Protect sensitive demographic information to prevent misuse and uphold ethical standards.
3. **Accountability**: Establish clear accountability for model outcomes and ensure compliance with fairness regulations and guidelines.

Conclusion

Detecting and analyzing demographic bias using machine learning is essential for building fair AI systems. Organizations can reduce demographic bias in their models by employing a range of detection techniques, analyzing bias sources, and implementing mitigation strategies. Continuous monitoring and ethical considerations will further support the development of equitable AI systems that serve all demographic groups fairly.

Social Inductive Biases for Reinforcement Learning

Incorporating social inductive biases into reinforcement learning (RL) can enhance agents' ability to learn and adapt within social contexts. These biases leverage knowledge about human behavior, social norms, and interactions, allowing RL agents to navigate complex environments more effectively. This approach is particularly relevant in applications like social robotics, collaborative environments, and interactive systems.

Key Concepts

1. **Definition of Social Inductive Bias**
   - Social inductive biases in RL are assumptions or prior knowledge about social interactions and behaviors that guide the learning process. They help RL agents understand and predict social dynamics, facilitating more human-like decision-making.
2. **Importance**
   - Integrating social biases can improve an agent's performance in tasks that require social reasoning, cooperation, or competition, enhancing its ability to function in human-centric environments.

Applications

1. **Social Robotics**
    - Robots that interact with humans can benefit from social biases that guide them in understanding human emotions, intentions, and social cues, leading to more effective communication and cooperation.
2. **Collaborative Learning**
    - In multi-agent systems, social biases can enable agents to learn from each other, facilitating knowledge sharing and joint problem-solving in shared environments.
3. **Game Playing**
    - RL agents can be designed to understand social strategies in competitive or cooperative games, improving their performance by recognizing and adapting to opponents' behaviors.
4. **Healthcare Applications**
    - Agents can be trained to consider social factors in healthcare settings, optimizing interventions based on patient behaviors and social networks.

Techniques

1. **Reward Shaping**
    - Design reward functions that incorporate social considerations, such as cooperation, fairness, and adherence to social norms, to encourage desired behaviors.
2. **Hierarchical Reinforcement Learning**
    - Utilize hierarchical structures that allow agents to learn social strategies at different levels, from basic interactions to complex social reasoning.
3. **Social Learning Mechanisms**
    - Implement mechanisms that enable agents to learn from the experiences of others, such as imitation learning or observational learning, to accelerate their learning process.
4. **Communication Protocols**
    - Develop communication strategies that allow agents to share information about their states, intentions, and plans, fostering cooperation and coordination.

Challenges

1. **Complexity of Social Norms**
   - Social norms can vary widely across cultures and contexts, making it challenging to encode these biases in a way that is universally applicable.
2. **Scalability**
   - Incorporating social biases may increase the complexity of the learning process, potentially slowing down convergence or requiring more computational resources.
3. **Dynamic Environments**
   - Social dynamics can change rapidly, necessitating continuous updates to the agent's understanding of social biases and interactions.
4. **Ethical Considerations**
   - Ensuring that RL agents behave ethically and do not perpetuate harmful biases or stereotypes is crucial, particularly in sensitive social contexts.

Conclusion

Integrating social inductive biases into reinforcement learning can potentially create more sophisticated, adaptable, and human-like agents. By leveraging knowledge of social dynamics, these agents can enhance their interactions in various applications, from robotics to healthcare. Ongoing research and collaboration across disciplines will be essential to refine these approaches and address the associated challenges, ensuring the responsible development of socially aware RL systems.

Program Synthesis for Social Recommendations

Program synthesis involves automatically generating programs from high-level specifications. In the context of social recommendations, this can mean creating algorithms that suggest content, connections, or actions based on user preferences and behavior. By integrating machine learning (ML) techniques, these systems can enhance user experience and engagement.

Key Concepts

1. **Social Recommendations:**
   - Refers to systems that suggest friends, groups, content, or actions to users based on their social networks and interactions.
   - Examples include recommending friends on social media, suggesting posts to read, or highlighting events to attend.
2. **Program Synthesis:**
   - The process of generating programs automatically to fulfill a specified requirement.
   - In social recommendations, this could mean creating recommendation algorithms that adapt to user behavior and feedback.

Applications

1. **Friend Recommendations:**
   - ML models can analyze user interactions, mutual friends, and shared interests to suggest new connections.
   - Program synthesis can be used to dynamically adjust the recommendation algorithms based on user feedback.
2. **Content Recommendations:**
   - Personalized suggestions for articles, videos, or posts based on user behavior, preferences, and social interactions.
   - Using reinforcement learning, the system can adaptively learn from user responses to improve recommendations.
3. **Event Recommendations:**
   - Suggesting social events based on users' interests, past attendance, and the preferences of their social circle.
   - Synthesis techniques can generate tailored algorithms that consider multiple factors, such as location and timing.

Techniques Used

1. **Machine Learning Models:**
   - **Collaborative Filtering:** Uses user-item interaction data to recommend based on similarities between users or items.
   - **Content-Based Filtering:** Recommends items based on features of the items themselves and the user's past preferences.
   - **Matrix Factorization:** Techniques like Singular Value Decomposition (SVD) can reduce dimensionality and uncover latent factors in user-item interactions.
2. **Deep Learning:**
   - **Neural Collaborative Filtering:** Combines deep learning with collaborative filtering techniques to enhance recommendation accuracy.
   - **Graph Neural Networks (GNNs):** Useful for modeling social networks and capturing complex relationships between users and items.
3. **Reinforcement Learning:**
   - Algorithms can learn optimal recommendation strategies through trial and error, adjusting based on user feedback and engagement metrics.

4. **Program Synthesis Techniques:**
    - **Specification-Based Synthesis:** Generates algorithms based on high-level specifications of desired outcomes, such as maximizing user engagement or satisfaction.
    - **Learning from Examples:** Inferring algorithms from a set of input-output pairs, where inputs are user data and outputs are desired recommendations.

Challenges and Considerations

1. **Data Privacy:**
    - Ensuring user data is handled responsibly and in compliance with privacy regulations is critical.
    - Implementing privacy-preserving techniques, such as differential privacy, can help protect user information.
2. **Bias and Fairness:**
    - ML models can perpetuate biases present in the training data. It's important to regularly evaluate and mitigate bias in recommendations.
    - Fairness in recommendations ensures that diverse user groups are represented and not disadvantaged.
3. **Interpretability:**
    - As recommendations become more complex, understanding how decisions are made is crucial for user trust and system transparency.
    - Techniques like explainable AI (XAI) can provide insights into how recommendations are generated.
4. **User Feedback:**
    - Continuously collecting and incorporating user feedback is essential for improving the accuracy and relevance of recommendations.
    - Adaptive algorithms should be designed to learn from this feedback in real-time.

Conclusion

Program synthesis combined with machine learning offers a powerful framework for developing social recommendation systems. By automatically generating tailored algorithms based on user behavior and preferences, these systems can significantly enhance user experience. Addressing challenges related to data privacy, bias, and interpretability will be crucial for the successful deployment of these technologies in social platforms. Collaborative efforts between researchers, developers, and users will drive innovation and improve the effectiveness of social recommendations.

Socially Guided Machine Learning

Socially guided machine learning (SGML) refers to the integration of social information and context into machine learning algorithms to improve decision-making, enhance user experience, and promote ethical outcomes. This approach leverages social norms, behaviors, and relationships to guide the learning process, particularly in environments where human interactions play a critical role. Here's an overview of how SGML can be implemented and its implications.

Key Concepts

1. **Social Context**: Understanding the environment in which users operate, including their relationships, community norms, and cultural factors.
2. **Social Influence**: Recognizing how individual decisions can be influenced by social interactions and group dynamics.
3. **Ethical Considerations**: Ensuring that machine learning applications align with societal values and promote fairness and inclusivity.

Applications of Socially Guided Machine Learning

1. **Personalized Recommendations**:
    - Leveraging social data (e.g., user interactions, preferences of similar users) to enhance the accuracy of recommendation systems, such as in e-commerce or streaming services.
2. **Sentiment Analysis**:
    - Analyzing social media and community feedback to gauge public sentiment about products, services, or policies, helping organizations to adapt their strategies accordingly.
3. **Social Robotics**:
    - Designing robots that can understand and respond to human social cues, enhancing human-robot interaction in settings like healthcare and education.
4. **Behavioral Prediction**:
    - Using social data to predict user behavior in online platforms, improving targeting strategies for marketing or interventions.
5. **Community Detection**:
    - Identifying and analyzing communities within social networks to tailor content and services to specific group needs.

Techniques Used

1. **Graph-Based Learning**:
    - Utilizing graph structures to represent social relationships and interactions, allowing for advanced analysis of social dynamics.
2. **Reinforcement Learning**:
    - Incorporating social feedback into reinforcement learning frameworks to guide agent behavior based on social norms and values.
3. **Natural Language Processing (NLP)**:
    - Analyzing social media content and interactions to extract insights about societal trends, opinions, and sentiments.
4. **Collaborative Filtering**:
    - Using collective preferences from a community to enhance recommendations, allowing for better personalization based on social influences.

Benefits of Socially Guided Machine Learning

- **Enhanced Accuracy**: Incorporating social context can lead to more accurate predictions and recommendations, as it reflects real-world dynamics.
- **Improved User Engagement**: Systems that understand and leverage social interactions can create more engaging and relevant experiences for users.
- **Ethical Alignment**: By considering societal norms and values, SGML can help mitigate biases and promote fairness in machine learning applications.
- **Informed Decision-Making**: Organizations can make better decisions by understanding the social implications of their products and services.

Challenges and Considerations

1. **Data Privacy**: Collecting and using social data raises significant privacy concerns, requiring careful management to protect user information.
2. **Bias and Fairness**: Social data may contain biases that can propagate through machine learning systems, necessitating strategies to ensure fairness.
3. **Dynamic Nature of Social Norms**: Social norms can change over time, making it crucial for models to adapt to evolving social contexts.
4. **Complexity of Social Interactions**: Capturing the nuanced dynamics of social relationships can be challenging and requires sophisticated modeling techniques.
5. **Integration into Existing Systems**: Implementing SGML approaches may require significant changes to current machine learning workflows and systems.

Conclusion

Socially guided machine learning represents a promising avenue for enhancing the relevance and ethical impact of machine learning applications. By integrating social context and dynamics into the learning process, organizations can create systems that are more aligned with human values, improve user experiences, and foster better decision-making. Ongoing research and collaboration across disciplines will be essential to fully realize the potential of SGML in various domains.

Election Exit Poll

Election exit polls are critical tools for predicting election outcomes and understanding voter behavior. By leveraging machine learning (ML), analysts can enhance the accuracy and efficiency of exit polling. Here's how ML can be applied to election exit polls:

Key Applications

1. **Voter Behavior Analysis**
   - **Predictive Modeling**: ML algorithms can analyze historical voting patterns, demographics, and survey responses to predict voter behavior in real time.
   - **Feature Importance**: Identifying key factors influencing voter decisions, such as socioeconomic status, education level, and local issues.
2. **Real-Time Data Processing**
   - **Dynamic Analysis**: Machine learning can quickly process incoming survey data, allowing for real-time updates and adjustments to predictions.
   - **Natural Language Processing (NLP)**: Analyzing open-ended responses to understand voter sentiment and concerns.
3. **Sampling and Weighting**
   - **Adaptive Sampling**: Using ML to determine the most

effective sampling strategies based on early voter turnout and demographics to ensure representative results.
   - **Weight Adjustment**: Automatically adjusting weights in the data to correct for bias and ensure that the poll reflects the actual electorate.
4. **Ensemble Methods**
   - **Combining Models**: Using ensemble techniques (e.g., bagging, boosting) to combine multiple ML models for improved accuracy in predictions.
   - **Model Validation**: Implementing cross-validation techniques to ensure robustness and minimize overfitting.
5. **Sentiment Analysis**
   - **Public Opinion Trends**: Analyzing social media and news sentiment to gauge public opinion leading up to and on election day, providing additional context to exit poll results.

Techniques Used

1. **Supervised Learning**
   - Algorithms like logistic regression, random forests, and support vector machines can be employed to classify voter intent based on demographic and survey data.
2. **Unsupervised Learning**
   - Clustering techniques (e.g., K-means) can identify distinct voter groups based on shared characteristics, informing targeted outreach and messaging.
3. **Deep Learning**
   - Neural networks can be utilized for complex pattern recognition in large datasets, especially in analyzing sentiment from unstructured data sources.
4. **Reinforcement Learning**
   - Could be explored for adaptive strategies in polling methodologies, optimizing the approach as new data comes in.

Benefits

- **Enhanced Accuracy**: ML models can improve the precision of predictions by analyzing more variables and identifying patterns that traditional methods might miss.

- **Faster Insights**: Real-time data processing allows for quicker adjustments to predictions based on incoming survey results.
- **Informed Decision-Making**: Better understanding of voter behavior and sentiments can aid political parties and candidates strategize and target their campaigns.

Challenges and Considerations

1. **Data Quality**: High-quality, representative data is crucial for training effective ML models. Inaccurate or biased data can lead to misleading results.
2. **Interpretability**: Many ML models can act as "black boxes." Ensuring that the results are interpretable and explainable is essential for trust among stakeholders.
3. **Ethical Considerations**: Handling voter data responsibly is crucial, especially with privacy concerns and the potential for misuse of information.
4. **Regulatory Compliance**: Adhering to laws and regulations surrounding polling and data usage is critical to avoid legal repercussions.

Conclusion

Integrating machine learning into election exit polling can significantly enhance the accuracy and responsiveness of predictions. By analyzing various data sources and employing advanced modeling techniques, ML can provide deeper insights into voter behavior and preferences. However, ensuring data quality, interpretability, and ethical handling of voter information remains paramount to the success and integrity of exit polls. As technology evolves, continuous refinement of ML methodologies will be essential to adapt to changing electoral dynamics.

www.ingramcontent.com/pod-product-compliance
Lightning Source LLC
LaVergne TN
LVHW052304200926
848481LV00002B/454
* 9 7 9 8 3 4 9 4 1 6 6 7 5 *